Back to the Country

MEMOIR OF A 1950s FARMER

CLEMENT T. "BUD" MERTENS

EDITED BY ELLEN M. MEYER

WillowBend
PRESS

Published by Willow Bend Press

Copyright © 1991-1994 by Clement T. Mertens
Copyright © 2022 by Ellen M. Meyer

Previously published as *My Story* in 1994

All rights reserved. No part of this book may be reproduced or transmitted in any form or by any means, electronic or mechanical, including photocopying, recording, or by any information storage and retrieval system, without permission in writing from the editor, except for the inclusion of brief quotations in a review.

ISBN-13: 979-8-3530-7820-3

Cover design by Ellen M. Meyer and Vicki Lesage

To my wife Ida, my love, and to those I love

Table of Contents

Introduction 1
Courtship, Marriage, and Babies 3
    My Early Life 5
    Looking for a Wife 7
    Courtship 14
    Wedding and Honeymoon 18
    Early Married Life 23
    Our First House 29
    Moving to Columbia 36
From Tire Sales to Hard Scrabble Farming 43
    Boarding Nephews 45
    Exploring Columbia 47
    Visiting Coal Mines 50
    Traveling Salesman 53
    Fun Day with Quentin 57
    Karen is Born 59
    Some Sad, Some Hard, and Some Amusing Things about Life in Columbia 63
    Deciding to Become Farmers 65
    Moving to the Country 68
    Working on Houses 71
    Buying a Farm 73
    Making the Farm Livable 77
Early Dairy Days 85
    Growing Wheat and Milking Cows 87
    Spreading Cinders in Winter 92
    Hauling Milk and Other Hard Work 95
    Getting New Cows 99
    Making Improvements 103

    Buying Farm Equipment 108

    Becoming Big Shots 112

Cows, Cows, and More Cows 119

    Driving Cattle 121

    Moving Up to Grade A Milk 124

    Remodeling Our House 126

    The Fall 129

    Throw in the Towel? 136

    Converting to Grade A Milk 140

    Fairs, 4-H, and Future Farmers 142

The Last of Our Dairy Cattle Years 147

    Earning Degrees and Winning Awards 149

    David Meets Carolyn 153

    Quality Over Quantity 156

    Getting Wired 162

    Getting Prettier 164

    David Marries Carolyn 166

    Goodbye, Dairy Farming 169

    The Freedom to Travel 173

From Cattle to Retirement 177

    Where's the Beef? 179

    Kicked by a Cow 181

    Walking with Sadie 183

    Hurt by a Calf 185

    Break for Baptisms 187

    Accident with the Combine 189

    Selling the Farm 194

Retirement 197

    Living in Town 199

    Replacing Rings 200

Seeing the Country 202

Serving the Community 204

Volunteering at Church 210

Aiding the Extension Service 214

Guardian Angels 219

Health Issues 221

Legal Woes 227

Speaking at the Field House 229

Epilogue 233

Acknowledgements 237

A Note from the Editor 238

Other Titles by Clement T. "Bud" Mertens 239

Table of Illustrations 240

Photo Credits 242

Introduction

CLEMENT T. "BUD" MERTENS, my great-uncle, was born in 1917 and wrote these stories between 1991 and 1994. I've collected his writings almost 30 years later to share with the world.

Bud wrote his tales in a serial fashion for our monthly family newsletter. My father, Quentin Veit, helped Uncle Bud in many writing projects. While going through Dad's computer files after his death, my sisters and I came across this manuscript. I have reorganized and edited the material to be more understandable to the general public. Some new illustrations have been added.

The early years of Bud's life are covered in his first book, *Raised in the Country*. His experiences during the Great Depression are the focus of his second book, *Hard Times in the Country*. *Serving My Country*, Bud's third book, tells about his Army days serving stateside during World War II. This is Uncle Bud's final book, where we follow Bud from his transition to civilian life from the Army through his adult years up until his retirement in 1978.

I didn't know Uncle Bud well, but after reading the story of his life, he's now a dear friend. It is my wish that after reading his story, you will come to regard Bud as a dear friend too.

Ellen M. (Veit) Meyer, editor

Courtship, Marriage, and Babies

My Early Life

I WAS BORN ON DECEMBER 20, 1917 and was raised in a small farming community in central Missouri. I come from a large family with lots of brothers and sisters. I was the youngest except for my adopted sister Louise who was often my partner in crime. We were also close with our extended family of aunts, uncles, cousins, and grandparents.

My mom had a "can-do" attitude about life, even though she had been crippled by polio when she was 18 months old. Her philosophy was that everyone was exactly what they wanted to be, that any problem anyone had was no one's fault but their own, and it was up to them to correct those problems. Dad was a talented carpenter and good with figures, although he had to give up carpentry after a bad accident where he almost lost his life. He ran the Mertens ferry across the Osage River for many years, then turned to farming. Although easygoing, he had high expectations for us kids. I'm proud to be my parents' son. We were a happy family and my parents were tops.

Everyone in our community seemed to have a nickname. I was called "Buben" which is German for rascal or scamp. I admit, I did get into trouble now and then. Somehow over the years Buben became Bud and that's what people still call me. Although some call me Clem.

My family had been torn apart by the Great Depression. My brother Felix died of meningitis at age 18 in 1930, and my father died in 1933 of Bright's disease. These untimely deaths left the whole family grieving, while still having to deal with the hard times of those days. My older sisters, Rose and Anna, were married and trying to survive with their own families. My older brothers Carl and Emil were dairy farmers struggling to get by, although Emil had owned and operated the Mertens ferry for a few years first. My mother tried to make a go at farming with my brother Everett, my sister Louise, and me after losing almost everything after Dad's death, but we just couldn't make it. Everett got a place of his own and Mom and Louise went to live with him. I was homeless for a while, staying with one family member or another.

After the Depression came World War II. I was called up to serve in the Army and left for Hammer Field in Fresno, California on May 28, 1942. I served stateside as mess steward at Hammer Field and then at Lemoore Army Air Field until my discharge on December 6, 1945. During this time, Emil took care of my cows and Everett took care of my team of horses. Mom died during my service and I didn't have a home to come back to after the war. I was lucky to have my family, the ones who were left, ready to help me and I was ready to help them. I moved in with Emil and his wife Cath and in return I helped brick their house and do other work for them.

Now I was back to civilian life, but I basically had to start all over again. I applied for many jobs but couldn't even get interviews, as the men who had been discharged earlier than me snapped them all up. I sold my cows to Carl and used the money to buy a new truck so I could get back into the hauling business. I traded my team of horses to Everett for his little worn out 600 Nash so I would have some transportation.

I now was ready to start my new life as a civilian.

Looking for a Wife

NOW THAT I WAS BACK HOME and still single, it was time to start looking for a wife and of course that called for a girlfriend. I did "look around" but it seemed every girl I had known was attached or married. I had hoped to have some assistance from my cousin Bill Mertens, but because his brother Ed was discharged and he could take Bill's place on the farm, the darn draft board took Bill into the Navy. I knew he had girls on his list but being away that did me no good. Darn.

Here Rose's daughter Lydia came to the rescue with her birthday club that she had asked me to join. I shied away from it, thinking this would be a poor place to find a mate as most members were kin in some way. I can tell you it wasn't easy since I was 28 years old and most women of my age were already married or "not wanted."

This birthday club was an old one started by the Butzers. Mrs. Butzer was a Mertens from Linn, Missouri. There must have been 40 people in this club and 34 were older than me or married. That left Bernice Butzer (Lydia's friend). She was divorced and rather plump.

But my prayers came to the rescue. Because it rained (so no lime hauling), I made a trip to Jefferson City. Growing up on a farm with rocks just waiting to stub a barefoot toe, I had learned to always look at the ground so as not to stumble over one. On this particular day I was walking on the south side of High Street heading east and just crossing Madison Street and speeding along with my 40-inch steps (which my dad had loved when I was plowing the field but my drill sergeant had hated when I was going through boot camp) and watching ahead where I placed them. Someone shouted, "Hey you!" and I turned to see Lydia and a very pretty girl that I had just passed right on by. (No wonder I never found a girl!)

Lydia said, "Uncle Bud, I want you to meet my cousin, Ida Mae."

Wow! Hot dog! For heaven's sake! And lots of other things!

"She just joined our birthday club," Lydia said, and after that it didn't take me long to join too. What luck.

Lydia and Ida

Let me explain this club, because after joining I found many friends and the best part was doing things as a group. Because of gasoline shortages they would rent a school bus owned by Geir from Russellville, Missouri. It was a new Dodge and it took the group on many outings that 24 worn-out cars could not afford to. It amounted to wiener roasts, horse riding farms, and trips to St. Louis, and most outings came about as the club had so many birthdays to celebrate. They just pooled the money and the one whose birthday was being celebrated got to plan the outing of his choice. It became quite a variety and was really more fun than I thought it would be.

1940s-era Dodge school bus

A side benefit of belonging to the club was I got used oil. Who would have thought I'd get something like that from being in a birthday club and who would have thought I'd be excited about it? But my old worn-out Nash guzzled oil by the gallon and I couldn't easily get new oil because of the post-war shortage, but I was able to get the used oil when the bus was done with it. Also due to the shortage, I couldn't fix the broken window of my right front door, but that didn't stop us running around in my overloaded car on the trips we didn't take by bus.

As for the members of the group, one of the young unmarried men was Ida's cousin, J. Paul Markway. The other unmarried man was a Butzer cousin, Ed Hartman, from New Bloomfield; a farm boy who also had ideas about Ida. Ida and Lydia were the only single girls and with Lydia being my niece that left her out. Ida's sister-in-law, Gerri Stockman, was also a member as her husband Willard still had not been discharged. Lydia had been dating Jerry Raithel and for some reason they broke up. Another young man just discharged from the Navy, Lee George Cremer, began dating her and along with Ida's brother Dave and his girlfriend. So we had our own little group.

Ida and me when we were dating

What griped me was that Ed Hartman attached himself to our group because of Ida. That made seven, up until Ida got rid of Ed. He was pretty hard to get rid of and I can't blame him for wanting Ida as I did too.

So here we went on trips with me furnishing the car and doing the driving with Ida sitting beside me and Ed Hartman sitting on the other side of her and neither of us with guts enough to tell the other he was not wanted. I can't say Ida led him on because at that time she thought she was spoken for by Elmer Rackers. Elmer was the son of Ted Rackers of Osage Bend and as a young boy, while I was living with Clarence and Anna, I walked to the Osage Bend school with him. He was a good friend of Ida's brother Willard and they dated together before he and Willard had to leave for the Army.

At that time Elmer and Ida were serious about each other, yet for some reason he kind of dropped her by not answering her letters but she felt after he was discharged he would come back. Here her brother Willard helped me as Gerri had roomed with Ida before they married and for some reason Gerri seemed to think I was a right sort of guy and told Willard so. I just could not get anything concrete out of Ida as she said she wanted to wait and be sure. Hellfire and damnation. I do believe that Willard told her I was the better choice but you have to remember that she was 21 here dating an old man of past 28. I do not know if Ed Hartman gave up or if she told him it was "no-go" but anyway he dropped out and then at least I did not have him to contend with. This whole thing amounted to being much tougher than the Army ever was.

Gerri and Ida

After Willard was discharged, he, because of Gerri, joined our group and we ran around together as he had no car either.

A couple of trips with that old Nash stand out. One time seven of us took it on an outing to Bagnell Dam. We took our dinner along with the one-gallon can of used oil and a gunnysack that was used as a window glass to keep out the cold and rain. I have to laugh now when thinking about it and Ed Hartman. He sat beside the window and the wind from driving flipped a steady mist of rain through that sack and in his face. To get further away from it he squeezed against Ida and she against me so that it was almost three of us under the steering wheel. Those were the days. I do not believe the little old car could have hauled us all if not for the large tires on the rear so it looked to be going downhill even while going up.

1941 ad for Nash 600

The second was a trip to the Palace Inn at Schuberts, the night club where the Taos-Osage City road crossed Highway 50. The highway crossed a bridge with a concrete railing just west of Schuberts. On this trip as we entered on the bridge a large white-face cow walked across the other end. To try missing her I swerved to the right while braking hard. We completely turned around on the bridge, not hitting either the cow or the bridge only we were heading back toward Jefferson City. That little old car leaned over so much that I thought we were laying on its side and had already turned over. It seemed odd but it just righted itself. I think that was because one of the girls sitting on her boyfriend's lap on the opposite side kept it from going over. You can believe this, the left rear tire lay over so much that the highway concrete ground the edge of the rim off. I can only say, "Thank God for the old truck tires" because if that tire had blown we would have gotten hurt and maybe bad. We were shook up pretty bad. When we got to the night club we told the gas attendant to call the Highway Patrol. He first asked, "Where did it happen?" and then said, "That was our cow!" and took off to get it penned.

Cow on bridge [1]

It got better for me as Ida began to forget Elmer Rackers and that gave me some hope but I was afraid she would say no if I asked her to marry me. I kind of hated to have to ask her every time for a date. She still talked about Elmer when I told her that I loved her and wanted to have her be my "steady."

Courtship

WE HAD FUN as our group and many times it was three o'clock in the morning before I arrived home and on those times I slipped in the window. Of course Emil got us up early to get the milking done so we could have breakfast and be in California, Missouri for work at half past seven o'clock. This continued throughout the summer. Emil and Evy spent every evening drinking beer at a local bar on the way home from lime hauling and I would just leave and when both Gladys and Cath saw me at home they knew that both of their husbands were goofing off and gave them hell and then both brothers gave me hell too.

More than anything I wanted my own home.

It was in early September 1946 when we went on a birthday party to Forest Park and the St. Louis Zoo, and after supper to the Highlands amusement park for the rides. We were driving home in the bus at about midnight and Ida and I were sitting together when I, not giving it a thought, asked Ida to marry me. I could hardly believe it when she said, "Yes, I will marry you." We were a happy pair that night and kidded on the way home and after getting off the bus and in the car we just sat and talked.

We found a piece of paper to measure Ida's finger for an engagement ring. I got both her engagement ring and wedding band and, just my luck, they were too small to go over her knuckle. I wanted to take them back to be made larger but she would not let me. So it took a lot of wetting her finger by sticking it in her mouth and the ring finally went on. These small rings caused a problem on the day we were married but I will get into that later. I never understood why she did not want me to have them made larger other than maybe she thought I might back out. With that ring I feel she knew that she loved me just as much as I did her.

One of the things we kidded about was that she said I had to ask her dad if it was okay for her to marry me. Knowing Roy Stockman, you can understand that this was like asking all over again and I was very afraid he would say no. Ida's dad was the oldest brother of my brother-in-law Elmer Stockman (Rose's husband). He was just the opposite of Elmer. Where Elmer couldn't care less, Roy couldn't care more. He was always full of fun like Elmer but I wondered whether he meant it as fun or not. You just kind of walked easy around him, being sure not to step on his toes. With Ida I also learned that she was not kidding about the asking so there is a little of Roy Stockman there too.

The evening I gave her the ring she said, "Let's go out and show it to Mom and Dad." They were sitting on the back porch railing, her mom next to the steps. Ida showed the ring to her mother and said, "Bud has something to ask you both." Oh hell! Ida's mother said she was happy for Ida and gave her permission but there sat Roy and that was another thing. He said he was happy for her too but added, "You sure as hell better take good care of her." Then he laughed, as did Ida, like it was a joke but to this day I still believe he meant it. Although Ida was working at the west-end shoe factory, I'm wondering if Roy wasn't sorry to give away all that she did at home and pass it on to me. Both Roy and Rose Stockman are now dead but both can be proud of their daughter.

Well! With all this done, I saw no reason to wait long before our wedding but here again Ida did. She wanted to wait until spring. She said, "After all we have only known each other for four months and what will people think." I really did not care what they thought and I felt we should marry as soon as possible. She finally gave in to my wants saying, "It will be quite a rush to get everything ready" and I will admit now that I had not thought of that. I suppose I was so much in love that I did not realize what I expected of her and her mother in rushing things so. The date she picked was her mother's birthday, November 9, 1946.

It's a good thing Ida knew how to sew as she made her wedding gown as well as the dresses of her attendants. I learned how hard it was to get ready as I could not find a suit to be married in. I had forgotten about the war shortage. I had a gray suit that I bought from Bill Mertens when he left for the Navy but it was ill-fitting, even after Cath and I altered it, and I didn't want to be married in that thing. I found a secondhand suit at Herman's Clothing Store. Mr. Herman told me it belonged to the widow of a serviceman who was killed in action and she wanted to sell it for $15. It was blue with a weave of light blue threads and looked great yet it was not a serge. It could not have been a better fit. I had to borrow a white shirt from Emil's brother-in-law, Joe Nilges, and a necktie from Emil. Today, thinking back, I'm surprised we ever made it.

Ida chose her sister Catherine as bridesmaid and her sister-in-law Gerri as attendant. I picked my friend Lloyd Imhoff (Louise's husband Ed's brother) as groomsman and Ida's brother Willard as best man. Poor Willard had trouble finding a suit also (no tuxedos in those days) so he borrowed a suit from his brother-in-law, George Wallendorf. I'm sure couples today think getting married is a hassle but I never dreamed of the problems we had. Really!

Me with Lloyd Imhoff

We were lucky in the fact that Ida and Lydia rented an apartment together at 404 Mulberry and Lydia gave her half to us. Lydia owned the bed and Ida had the breakfast set. How to get a bedroom set. Somewhere through a friend at work Ida found a used set for the price (at that time high) of $90 but it was a beauty and of such a good quality that we still use it today. We shared the Tripp's refrigerator as they were our landlords.

After his discharge Willard purchased an old 1936 four-door Pontiac. It had worn front spindles so it looked spraddle-legged but at least it had a glass in each window so we chose it as our wedding car. It certainly was not a limousine but it got us to church, to English's Studio for the picture taking (not allowed to take pictures in church in those days), and to our apartment at about nine o'clock that evening to change clothes and walk to the bus station to leave for our honeymoon to Kansas at ten o'clock. We had no dance. We had threats of a shivaree or of kidnapping Ida but here Roy again put a stop to that. We'd heard the story of Bill Ottman, who owned the Twin Oaks clubhouse on our farm in the 1920s, who had his wife taken as a prank and they were kept apart for five days. Fortunately it seems everyone was just as afraid of old Roy as I was and so we didn't have to worry about anything like that happening to us.

Wedding and Honeymoon

THE DAYS AND WEEKS leading up to the wedding were busier than I thought possible. We were both working at the time, on top of all the wedding plans. Many times since then I asked Ida, "How did we get it all done?" But somehow the great day came.

When I told my sister Rose that Ida and I were getting married she said, "You don't know how lucky you are to get that girl." At that time I thought so also but I really learned how lucky I was throughout the next 47 years. Thank you God.

Okay! My friend Lloyd came in from St. Louis so I rented a double room out at Warwick Village for him and me to stay overnight. Several of my friends along with Willard and Ida's half-uncle, Norbert Stockman, planned a little bachelor party with wine and ham sandwiches. The festivities had to be over by midnight because at that time you could not eat or even drink water after midnight before going to Communion.

I must have eaten a tainted ham sandwich because I awoke at about three o'clock with the worst case of cramps and was really sick. By morning it had gotten worse, with me spending a lot of time in the outhouse, wondering how I was going to get through the wedding. (It was here that I learned Gerri also had that worry as she became pregnant after Willard came home from the war and she had to fight off morning sickness.) Yet both of us made it through.

After Father Baughman blessed the rings, he gave me the one for Ida and told me to put it on her finger while saying the "I thee wed" and that small ring hardly got past the first knuckle, let alone the second. I really worked at it, not knowing I was shaking my head back and forth in trying to get it on, and finally gave up with it on the end of her finger. Somehow she got it on but when we got out of church everyone kidded me about the head shaking, asking if I thought I was making a mistake.

Our wedding

Poor Gerri! She barely made it out of church before having to vomit and that had to be in a handkerchief and then buried or burned.

Wedding party: Lloyd Imhoff, Willard Stockman, me, Ida, Catherine Stockman, Gerri Stockman

As for me, I can tell you I was "pinching back" and barely made it to the house and the outhouse. Well I made that trip about 20 times that day and when we left on the bus for our honeymoon I made it to each bus stop and was thankful they made about 10 stops before reaching Kansas City. We sat in the first seat, right behind the driver, and when we stopped I hit the toilet and Ida kept the driver from leaving without me.

Since my junky Nash was in no way dependable enough for the 460-mile round-trip, we rode a Missouri Pacific bus. It was a slow bus then because of poor tires so it was breakfast time when we reached Kansas City. I didn't feel like eating so Ida suggested chocolate milk and that did help stop those runs. Would you believe that we left Jefferson City at 10 o'clock at night on Saturday and didn't arrive at Cunningham, Kansas until three o'clock on Monday morning?

Many years earlier, my Aunt Fern had inherited (probably from her parents) six acres of land in Cunningham. During the Depression, they lost their farm and moved to the six acres that had a nice home and they built an early little cabin type motel. During World War II they converted the cabins to housing for servicemen from Salina Air Base. They did very well in the motel business. Knowing Ida and I were to be married in November, they invited us to spend our honeymoon with them.

We had to get Uncle Gus and Aunt Fern out of bed when we arrived at their little motel which was right on U.S. Highway 54. They took us to our cabin and said, "Get up when you want. There are eggs and bacon in the refrigerator for your breakfast and after we'll show you around."

They had little two-room cabins that they fixed as apartments for married soldiers stationed at Smokey Hill Air Base and, as the war was over, gave us one of them. The cabin had a kitchen so we just lived as if we were at home. When we were ready we would go to their house and then they would show us around and visit kin and old friends of Mom and Dad who migrated to Kansas during the wheat shocking days.

Cousin Don Huhmann in front of honeymoon cabins

Of course this could not last forever so it was back to work for both of us.

Early Married Life

IN DECEMBER we were not hauling lime, as that was a seasonal job for spring and fall. Willard and I were working for Willard and Ida's dad cleaning up tree tops that were left from the Derkum family, who were selling stave bolts that were used to make oak barrels. (To keep things clear I am going to call Ida's father "Dad" from now on.)

Stave bolts being unloaded from a wagon [2]

Dad had a contract to take all the ends that came off the stave bolts when they were sawed to even the length of the stave. A stave bolt is a section of a log to be cut into staves, which are then used to make wooden barrels, such as those used for aging whiskey. These end pieces from the stave bolts worked better in a furnace than did wood of stove length but there were people who wanted wood of "stove-wood" length. These Derkum tree tops worked well for that, hence our winter job.

I always liked to hunt and, since I never had the chance during my Army years, I wanted to buy a semi-automatic 12-gauge shotgun. Again because of the shortage none were available. I had put my name in at every hardware store and was just waiting. Ida found a man who worked at Montgomery Ward who said he had a used one that he would sell for $90. At that time, if available, they would have sold for less than $50. This guy had a little black market going but she bought it for me for Christmas.

Elmer, Willard, and I planned a rabbit hunt on New Year's Day. Of course it was cold and we could get nothing started but the truck and went to church in it. Elmer called saying it was too cold for him but Willard and I decided we would go anyway. We planned on hunting at Tipton as there were always lots of rabbits there but with snow on the ground we never found any. On the way home I remembered a little bottom field by a lime quarry we worked at many years before and decided to try there. I don't think it was even 15 acres but the two of us got 92 rabbits and two quail.

We were happy about all the meat we were going to have for the summer as we and Willard and Gerri had rented the top freezer locker in the old Igloo Locker plant. It was the cheapest but you had to use a step ladder to reach it. So we dressed rabbits until midnight and wrapped them in the old brown wrapping paper (no freezer wrapping paper in those days).

Mom and Dad Stockman gave their son and daughter a fat hog each for Christmas (but we had to help butcher) so we also had sausage, jowl, backbone, ribs, and head meat stored and were ever so happy about it. However, by June the meat was so strong, almost spoiled, that you could not eat it so we tried it with gravy but that didn't help either so we had to throw it away. Thank God that we had taken the rest of the hog out to Clarence and Anna for Clarence to cure with his faithful salt cure. At least we had that meat to eat. What was so disappointing was we'd been conserving it to make it last, only to throw all that good eating away. How dumb we were. So you people of today be thankful that we of our day pioneered freezer wrapping paper.

Ida and I decided to sell the little Nash since we could use the truck for transportation. We sold it to a nice black man for $250 and this was more than I'd given Evy for it as I had traded two horses that were valued at $100 each. Ida had $300 in savings bonds and with my savings and the money from the car it amounted to $1,200, so we thought we should build a home as our two-room apartment was somewhat cramped.

Ida's mother had inherited 40 acres of land from her father's estate and we wanted to buy a couple of acres of it on the southeast corner but she just gave it to us. We had Chester Platt plot it out for us and when he had it ready I borrowed Carl's new Studebaker truck and hauled my boss's little D-2 highlift to dig the basement. Before that I went to my friend Frank Railton to see if he would make a low interest VA loan for us. He said he would, but wanted us to know that, as he said, "These things take forever to get through government red tape." His advice was to go to a lumber yard, a concrete company, and a contractor and explain to them that the loan would not clear soon and find out if they would be willing to wait for the loan. So I went to Nanson Readymix (now Cole County) and Scruggs-Guhlman Lumber and both agreed and so we were on our way since we intended to hire kinfolks and friends and do most of the work ourselves.

We had no idea what this would amount to.

In our haste we exposed ourselves to a problem that came about through our new neighbors. They were Mr. and Mrs. Joe Luebbert, who had bought the land across the road from our lot on the Prenger estate. In the Markway home place for as long as was remembered, it was thought that the county road was the line between the Markway and Prenger farms. To be on the safe side and for the loan, we thought we should have our land surveyed and found that the road, with an S Curve and fenced on both sides for those many years, was not the property line. We found that Mom and Dad owned two and a half acres on the west side of the road on the north end, farmed and pastured by Mr. Luebbert, and that Mr. Luebbert in turn owned a 0.05 acre strip of land right in front of the home we were ready to build. In talking it over with Mom and Dad and Mr. Luebbert, it was decided to make the center of the road the property line and they would just exchange the land even up. Since Mr. Luebbert would get the advantage, it was thought to be a deal.

Mr. Luebbert had borrowed the money for the land from Ben Berhorst of Freeburg and had to contact him to see if the agreement would be okay. It was here that Mr. Berhorst put a bug into Mr. Luebbert's ear thinking that, since we had already started the home, he could hold us up for the great expense of the deeds and abstract. This created some contention between Mr. Luebbert and Dad, and knowing Dad, I thought we would have one hell of a fight on our hands.

We had Mr. F.E. Ross, the Cole County Engineer, do the surveying and write up the Deeds of Trust. When he got them finished both parties went to his office to sign them and as luck would have it Mom and Dad went first. When Mr. and Mrs. Luebbert signed theirs, Mr. Ross gave them both deeds saying, "You can just drop them by the Stockman's," which he did not do.

It was at this point that the expense came up and produced a fighting angry Roy Stockman. I went to Mr. Ross and asked him why he gave Dad's deed to the Luebberts because he would not give Ida's dad's deed to him. His answer was, "You mean that SOB did not give you the deed? I'll tell him that I will just resurvey the road and give you the land he has in front of your house." Knowing that Mr. and Mrs. Luebbert were going to be our neighbors we did not want to be fighting so we decided to tell Mr. Luebbert that we would pay the expense. I could also then understand the mortgage lender's concern about Mr. Luebbert.

Here again Ida and I made another mistake. We decided to go ahead and drop the argument regardless. Mr. Ben Prenger had a disabled son who would never have been able to take care of himself so Ben and his wife willed the farm to that son so the money from the farm sale would take care of him. This left out his other children and they decided to break that will. The entire court action was on the abstract because they did succeed in breaking that will. It cost Ida and me over $200 for the abstract alone and that made our free lot the most expensive lot on record. Remember, it would not have sold for $100 at the time. At least we could go forward, but I would call this learning the hard way.

We planned to hire kinfolks for the carpenter work and use our savings to pay them. So it came about that my brothers-in-law, Clarence Veit, Elmer Stockman, and Willard Stockman, and my brothers Emil and Everett helped us build our home. We must have done a good job as it is still in use today. Of course the greatest amount of work was done by Ida and me and that was every evening after work and up to midnight.

Emil, Cath, Ida, and me

Ida's uncle, Frank Markway, did the plastering so it was a nighttime job installing window trim and hanging light fixtures. I am really proud of my wife that, although pregnant, she worked right along with me. I call to mind the evening of September 10 when we worked until 10 o'clock hanging the living room light fixture and then went to the basement using wallpaper paste to completely wrap the heat pipes of the furnace with asbestos. (According to today's standards I am surprised that we are still here. After the great asbestos flap, we should both be dead from lung cancer.)

We were both tired that night as we headed back to the apartment. At about one o'clock Ida woke me and said our baby was ready to be born. Although tall, Ida only weighed 105 pounds and she certainly showed her pregnancy.

After we arrived at the hospital, she asked me to go for her mother and it was then I knew she was afraid. Well, Mom and I sat in the waiting room until almost eight o'clock before our son David was born. He weighed eight pounds and nine ounces and gave his mother quite a time in being born. Those days the mother stayed in the hospital eight days.

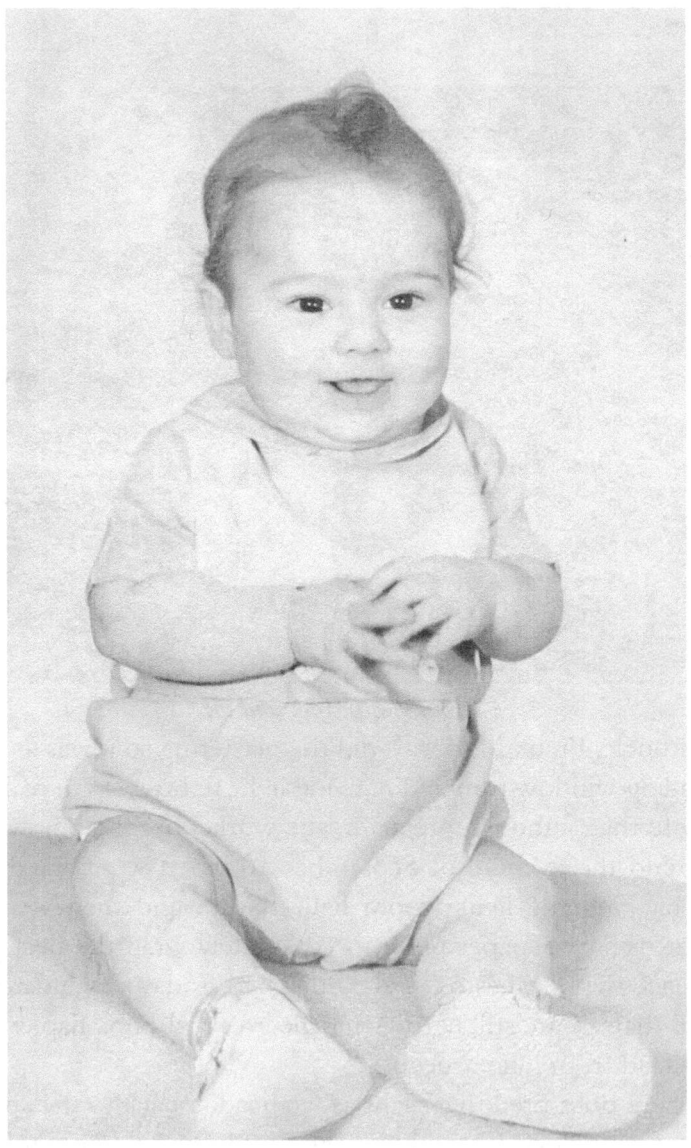

Baby David

Our First House

AS A YOUNG PERSON you have many dreams and to accomplish those dreams one can get too eager and so it was with us. You just never think that there may be a problem ahead until it comes like a slap in the face.

As we were working along with the home and I was hauling lime we thought we had the world by the tail. But one day we learned that, due to reducing the war debt, Congress decided lime was not that essential to the country and farmers and so cut it from the budget. That meant an expensive truck and no job. Thank God the truck was paid for. Again our prayers helped and that came about in an odd way.

We rented our apartment from an aged couple by the name of William Tripp who were devout Baptists yet thought a lot of us Catholics. They thought a lot of Ida and through our marriage that included me.

Their son Glenn married a Catholic girl by the name of Rackers and joined the Catholic Church for her. When we knew him, Glenn was a Navy lieutenant commander. He had just returned from many years as a war prisoner of the Japanese having been captured at Bataan and survived the Death March, a hundred-mile march without food, water, or sleep. Those who collapsed along the way were killed on the spot. Survivors of the march were kept in a prison camp and fed barely enough for only the hardiest to survive. He was a tall man who weighed 185 when captured and when liberated weighed only 89 pounds. He told of eating worms, grasshoppers, and butterflies to survive yet he never let it get him down. He also told how it was his Catholic faith that carried him through and that made a great impression on his parents. I wonder where Glenn is today. He remained in the Navy. He and his wife had three children.

Glenn and Dorothy Tripp's wedding photo

The Tripps also had a discharged son who fought in the South Pacific and his name was Charles. When Charles was discharged, he took a job with the General Tire Store in Jefferson City. Because of making up for the tire shortage during the war, they were very busy. When Charles learned about me with no work he recommended me to them and I applied and got the job. My pay was $41.60 per week and that was for six days including overtime. This worked out great for Ida and me as it was on the way to Wardsville so she would pick me up (yes she could drive a truck, a child of Roy Stockman could do anything it seems) after making sandwiches that we would eat on the way out and then we would work on our home.

There were five men working in the shop and I was the tire changer along with Charles. One of the five, the shop foreman, was Frank Puetz and a guy who was not asleep and for that again I am thankful. He would have me "buff" the old tread off the tires for recapping when I was not busy otherwise. As I was always willing to work, that helped me in the near future. He also taught Charles and me how to "lay" repairs in tires that had breaks, making them almost like new. He taught both of us how to recap tires too.

After David was born we moved to our new home. Ida did lots of painting and I with a wheelbarrow hauled lots of dirt to level the yard.

Our first house

By the way, we were working on our home on the Saturday after the tornado that destroyed St. Thomas and it did us a favor. There was a thorny locust tree in our front yard that I dreaded having to remove. The wind blew it out of the ground and I used Dad's tractor to drag it away. What was odd was that our window sashes held in the frame with only a single nail and the wind never blew a one out. Luck was with us as we had not put on the window trim as yet. Had a place for our garden too. Thus ended our year of 1947 and me with the great old age of just turned 30.

Me, Ida, and David

As 1948 began we still did not have a refrigerator even with our name in at every appliance store in Jefferson City. We were lucky to even have a stove to cook on. We got that through Ida's great-uncle Sam Hager who, with her dad's cousin, Sam Jr., had a bottled gas business. We thank God for that. In fact we almost worked God to death. We sure asked Him for lots of help.

I forgot to tell you that in the fall of 1947 I was best man for my friend Lloyd Imhoff's wedding in St. Louis. His sister Gertrude married Albert Stimel. Albert and his brother Frank both worked for General Motors and Lloyd married Frank's daughter, Darlene. Messed up like

Ida and me. Darlene, like Ida, had to now call her uncle her brother-in-law. Lloyd had another sister and she married Ralph Smallwood who, in our Tipton days, managed the Piggly Wiggly food chain store in Jefferson City. (This was the first self-service store chain.) Anyway, this chain sold out to Kroger and he lost his job. Lucky for Ida and me we met Ralph again at Lloyd's wedding and told him about our not being able to get a refrigerator. He was now working for an appliance store in Jefferson City and he explained how everybody was in the same spot. Of course they, like us, had their names entered everyplace.

Ida and Darlene

Ralph told us that people bought the first available appliance and when you called their name you found they already had one. So they called the next person in line. He said when that happens I will just put your name in that place and call you as the next up. Would you believe that happened within two months? We admit it was cheating but we really needed a refrigerator because of David although Ida nursed all her babies. Got it for $94 too. Thank you, Ralph, you were a great friend when in need.

Some other things took place the year of 1948 and one was a hell of a scare. Tire production began catching up with demand so there were rumors of layoffs and since Charles and I were last hired we figured we would soon be out of a job. Again our prayers were answered because, as Frank Puetz said, it was the "complainers" who were fired and Charles and I kept our jobs.

The second thing was that Ida helped her dad make 900 gallons of molasses that he sold to the State Penitentiary. The sons had the nasty job of stripping the cane and cutting and squeezing it. I always hated that job as a farm boy myself. Ida and Dad cooked the cane and placed it in gallon containers. Ida dropped David off with Grandma (Ida's mom), nursing him when he got hungry, and after we got off work she came home smelling like milk and honey. She sure was a "sweet" thing because we needed that money too. She had quit her shoe factory job some months before David was born.

The third thing was that the concrete company and lumber company began giving me a hard time about the money and with the VA loan still not approved. Again I went to my friend Mr. Railton and asked what we could do to speed things along. He said, "You can't, so we will just make you a loan to pay them and we will make the loan for the home when we receive approval." The surprising thing was that only a short time later it was approved and we got that straight. We only had to borrow $5,000 and that gave us about $500 to help replace our savings we had spent. Besides, Ida wanted a sewing machine.

Our house payments were $47.54 per month. My pay was $166.40 per month so that left us $118.86 for everything else and one of those was a hospital and doctor bill. By the way, Dr. Ossman, our family doctor who treated my appendicitis when I was 20, was our doctor and he did, like the hospital, take payments. Now after these bills were paid, Ida wanted a Maytag washing machine like her mother's. She was doing our laundry, helping Mom with hers at the same time. We lucked out here as we received a call from Montgomery Ward that our name had come up so we purchased one of theirs instead of Ida's cherished Maytag. Got it for $47 and it lasted until after we moved to the farm. Washed a lot of dirty clothes too.

During this time Ida's dad sold Grade A milk to St. Louis and was continually being degraded. Each time it happened it meant repainting, hauling manure, and everything else to satisfy the St. Louis milk inspector. Of course Ida helped here too. That worked out fine because she could raid his milk cans for the milk we used at home (funny thing, that milk didn't satisfy the inspector but it didn't hurt us any). We learned that you had to stay on the good side of these sort of guys and Dad never did learn that and was always having words with him and thus was always in trouble. He just couldn't stop being Roy Stockman.

Also the farmers got to their Congressman and thereby got the lime again and we were called back for hauling. Ida and I discussed this and came up with the idea that since I was one of the ones not being fired from my job it would be chicken of me to quit. It helped make the decision that we would never be sure of Congress and may have to face up to the same thing at a later time.

When Emil learned that I wasn't coming back to lime hauling he asked if he could buy our truck (on payments, that is) and we quickly agreed. We had some extra money coming in and that was necessary since we now had to have a car. (Always something.) Well those darn cars were still hard to find but we heard through the grapevine that a Mr. Sappenfield of Sappenfield and Sims Plumbing and Guttering Company might sell his car. I got that information while servicing one of their service pickups. I contacted the old man and found that he would sell his 1936 Dodge four-door sedan for $125 but that the motor was not the best. It was cheap enough so we purchased it, thinking of having Ida's brother Dave overhaul it. He in turn worked for a Mr. Ortmeyer at a Skelly Station and was eating dinner with us while we lived at the apartment. Mr. Ortmeyer called saying they thought the car had a "flat" crankshaft and recommended a rebuilt motor. Since the body of the car had always been shedded it still looked great so we had the rebuilt motor installed and that turned out to be a very good car.

Moving to Columbia

THE YEAR OF 1948 was a full year for us as General Tire had a commission warehouse in Columbia and they wanted Charles to transfer there. He did not want to make the move so they offered me the position. My current wages were $166.40 per month for a six-day week and this job would pay a flat $250 per month with every other Saturday off. Ida and I decided I should take that job and drive back and forth.

It didn't take us long to learn that I was now working an 11-hour day to do eight hours of work. It took one and a half hours of driving from Wardsville to my job on the north side of Columbia and through the full length of town. Snow and ice didn't help either. I can remember one full week of driving with chains as that winter we had our share of ice. The old Dodge hung right in there.

Two things came up to cause us to move to Columbia. First was the manager who thought I might get tired of driving and want to change jobs so he urged me to look at a home in a new subdivision on the extreme north of town. He learned about this as we were doing the developer's tire work and thought that would help the developer too. Ida and I drove up on a Sunday and gave it a look. This suited us as it was far out and would be almost like living in the country.

The second was that Ida learned she was expecting again. She didn't want to change doctors but Mr. Whitely, my big boss, said he would give us a good recommendation. So we proceeded to buy and, as I remember, it was in early September 1949. Just as soon as we learned the loan had gone through we planned to sell our home. We moved as soon as we could and Ida, through my friend there Dave Morris and his wife, got her doctor; they recommended their doctor who was an older man named Dr. Baker.

Our house in Columbia

I do have to admit here, as a married man, I was "running about in a circle" and no way near as organized as I was in the Army. Yet, after we moved, a new home sewing machine became available along with a living room set for our home and Ida's dream.

Now with another on the way and with David getting too long for the baby bed, which he would have to give up anyway, Ida wanted to buy a spindle bed. We ordered one from Sears Roebuck that came three weeks later by way of the Wabash Railroad. That bed moved to many apartments while the kids were going to college and is now in Wisconsin in our son David's home. When we visit them, we sleep in it. It got bunged up a little through the many moves yet still sleeps good. The only reason Ida gave it away was she received her grandmother Markway's antique bed that is worth thousands to her today. It had sat for many years in her mother's chicken house as "who would want such a bed?" and Ida did. The funny thing about this bed is that it is of solid oak and the headboard almost reaches to the ceiling. We have a 1904 Sears Roebuck catalogue and it is listed there for the great amount of $4.95. Ida stripped it and refinished it and I have an idea that there may be a fight among her children as to who gets it.

Ida's antique bed, now used by great-grandson Quentin [3]

This calls to mind that when Ida's dad died, two of his sons wanted his Remington 12-gauge shotgun. The one who never hunted had the money and the son who liked to hunt didn't. I could see this hurt Fred, my favorite brother-in-law.

When we made our will, I asked our attorney how we could get around this sort of thing. His suggestion was to write in the will that any child who wanted a certain thing could buy it for what it was worth to them and take it out of their part of the inheritance. That way they could be in competition and go as far as they wished and not have to drop out because of shortage of money.

When we moved to Columbia, we had to sell our home. When Ida's parents gave us the lot they said if we ever sold it to give another child the first chance. Thinking we would live there forever that hadn't bothered me but I do believe now that I would not accept something given under those conditions. "Never lend money to a member of the family."

We immediately got a buyer in a young couple by the name of Vogel. Then Ida's brother Dave who, after marrying, lived in an apartment and had no money wanted it. Our asking price was $7,500. That amount would cover the cost and our work and give us back our money to buy our home in Columbia. We had borrowed the whole amount and wanted to reduce it.

Ida's brother tried with his meager means and the advice to him was to borrow the down payment elsewhere and assume my 4% VA loan. But he just could not come up with the money, so good-hearted Ida and I decided to carry the amount with a promise of a monthly payment plus his paying the $47.54 monthly payment to the Exchange National Bank. This he sure promised to do.

He kept up the payments to the bank but for some reason, probably because of being kin, he did not think to pay us. I chickened out here, so when he got behind it was Ida who would go down to hit him up. What really burned her was she still had no sewing machine and when she went after the money found that Dave had given his wife Wanda a new Singer sewing machine. Dave's Confirmation sponsor was my brother-in-law Elmer and that must have "rubbed off" on him as he did business just like Elmer did.

Dave still had not paid us until we purchased our farm in 1954, and at that time it got to the point where we demanded it. What really bothered Ida was that after we bought our little two-door Plymouth he and Wanda came out with a four-door, two-tone Pontiac.

We wanted to buy a Deluxe Chevrolet Sedan and they were now available. When the salesman said he wanted to drive our old Dodge to the company for appraisal and came back with an offer of $85, that put it out of reach as the Chevy cost $1,857 and we could not make the extra as a down payment. I asked the man if he could do better but as we were now in the Korean War his answer was, "If you don't want it I can always sell it to someone else" and I haven't owned a Chevrolet since.

Cars were still scarce so we tried Ford. It cost $1,779 but we could only get a flat-head six and I remembered that motor came out in 1940 and was problematic. So we went to a Chrysler dealer and he told us he could not even talk with us because they were having a strike. We had to forget about a new car.

In the meantime one of the field men at General Tire by the name of Byrul Smarr got picked up for speeding and reckless driving three times so the insurance company demanded he be fired. The pay here was a flat $250 plus 10% commission and his loss was my gain as they gave me his job. This was a job that "the harder you worked the more you made" and by working I did well.

Then too one evening the Chrysler dealer brought a little two-door Deluxe Plymouth and said for me to take it home to show Ida. When I got home with it the dealer had called Ida and told her to take it out for a drive and bring it back in the morning when I came to work. We decided to buy it if we could make a trade. It was green.

Theodore, Karen, and David on the Plymouth

In those days they used one car to tow another to the dealer from the factory and I noticed by the clamp marks that this car had done the towing. He had the towed car, which was tan, so I told him we did not like the green color. I took him to the parking lot and showed him the old Dodge and he just slammed the doors and didn't even start it, yet offered us $185 on a trade-in. Since the Plymouth only cost $1,529 we now had our new car. From then on, we bought Chrysler products—17 of them to be exact—and found each one to be tops, even after being told by Dave Morris, the Stockmans, and the Mertens what fools we were. In 1988 we bought a Mercury Sable as Chrysler then did not make a car with a motor large enough to pull a trailer.

Our son Theodore was born on Easter Sunday morning April 9, 1950 and even after 43 birthdays it has never fallen on Easter Sunday again. He was here for his birthday and it was on Saturday and that was as close as it had ever been, within one day.

Baby Theodore

When I took the field man job, I got the company to hire Rose and Elmer's son Earl Stockman in my place. His nickname was "Boob" and so far as I go the best son they had. He was about 18 years old then and he lived with us. He took a bus back and forth when going home. The poor kid wanted a car so I signed the note for him to buy a 1936 standard-six Chevrolet and was he ever proud. After that I believe he would have done anything I asked him to. He later joined the Navy and drowned while in the service. I think that hurt Ida and me just as if he had been a son.

From Tire Sales to Hard Scrabble Farming

Boarding Nephews

OUR NEPHEWS Clarence Veit, Jr. and Harold Stockman stayed with us while going to college and later nephew Quentin Veit did too.

I remember how Quentin used to ride to school with me when I went to work and how sometimes we would turn right and go past all the fraternity houses, especially when it was raining. And I remember the time he didn't drop off at school and just rode with me on my route and how we caught heck when we got back at about midnight. We forgot to tell Ida that Quentin wouldn't be coming home from school at the regular time and she was worried out of her mind. Ha! Ha! Those were the days. What we thought was fun and all. Many years from now all of you can write your memoirs calling this sort of thing to mind from your days of the past.

Since we now had two sons and two boarders (no dogs or cats, they came from the neighbors), I will call us all the Mertens family. These were the days of ice cream, "pts" and "qts" (which is what we called ice cream so the kids would not know what we were talking about), if we could scrape that amount of money together. When we were really flush we would have our Miller High Life beer. No parties in those days, so a bottle of beer was about as high as our life could get.

One of the great points of that life was Quentin's fried potatoes. I got us both in dutch when I asked Ida, "Why can't you fry potatoes like Quentin does?" I didn't blame Ida for losing her cool but for a while Quentin was afraid he would be thrown out of the house. Oh well, I did like fried potatoes. Since my job was one where I had to spend two nights a week away from home those guys acted as bodyguards for my family and I will always appreciate that.

We charged our boarders $5 for room and meals for five days, Sunday evening through Friday afternoon. I'm sure it was not enough to make them much poorer or us much richer. Quentin would take a bus to Jefferson City on Friday evening and work with his dad and Joe Schmidt on Saturday for $1.25 per hour. His eight hours earned him $10 which paid his bus fare both ways, our $5, and left him a little over for incidentals like cigarettes. As part of the deal, he had to help Ida around the house while our daughter Karen was little, doing dishes and also some cooking and washing for a time. The cooking led to the incident mentioned above. Our arrangement was a bargain for all of us.

Exploring Columbia

I MADE TWO GREAT FRIENDS while working in Columbia. One was Dave Morris and the other Leon Bea. Leon was an older man (that is, older than Dave and me). We all liked to hunt and one time we had quite an experience while on a rabbit hunt. This was about 12 miles northeast of Columbia and alongside a large creek.

We were looking for a place to stop and Dave said, "This looks like a good place." Well we didn't get many rabbits there but we did get to see things none of us had ever seen before. There was quite a bottom along the creek with weeds as high as trees and you couldn't hit a rabbit if it stood at the end of the gun barrel. What we found was an abandoned bridge. It was quite a sturdy bridge but the floor had already rotted away. From the bridge we found a roadway. In thinking about it now, I believe it may have been a railroad right-of-way.

To get away from the weeds we followed this road toward the hill and there came to a hole in the hill. We found it to be an old coal mine. We ventured in as far as we could and, noting the rotting beams that held the ceiling up, got the hell out of there. We continued along, hoping for rabbits, and found another such hole. This one had two small rails running into it with a little four-wheel cart with a rotting wooden bed that would have held about four full wheelbarrows of coal. I suppose it was either pushed by a man or pulled by a small mule. By this time we were doing more exploring than hunting since we came upon a house sitting up on the hill. It was a T-shaped house with a front porch and with the door swinging back and forth so we decided to look it over. Many leaves had blown in so we could tell it had not been lived in for many years.

We took it upon ourselves to check it out and, believe me, it was eerie. It seemed as we explored that a ghost could begin speaking to us. All the furniture was just as it was left those many years past. It was a small house with a bedroom and living room in front and the kitchen extended toward the rear. The bedroom had a bed and it was made up just as if it was left only that morning and what was really weird, in all those years it had not been disturbed. The living room had the usual furniture but also had a piano and when you hit a key it still played. It looked just like the piano we had at home when I was a kid, an upright, but was not a self-player like ours which had rolls that played. There was a scarf across the top of it that had turned yellow from age and had little gold tassels hanging from each end. Laying on top of that scarf were issues of the Saturday Evening Post from the 1917-1918 years. We spent our hunting time looking through these and it was amusing because they were just full of advertisements and most were of cars.

You could buy a Chevrolet Baby Grand (this was a large car and I did not know that Chevy had made one of that size) that sold for $1,000. I suppose that was the why of the Grand name because there was also a 490 like the one Dad had as a 1915 model and it sold for $490. A Stutz Bearcat sold for over $1,300 and a Maxwell runabout could be purchased for $435. Model Ts were in the range of $360 to $400.

I could go on for a week with the things we read in those magazines so I will move on to the kitchen. It looked like it was ready for a meal. The roof had been leaking and the back porch was rotting away, but from it you could go into the cellar and we did, only to find it full of canned food. The food was canned with the old zinc lids and there was fruit, beets, and green beans. The cans sitting next to the door had frozen and burst but those that had not I think could have been eaten. The odd thing was that, although there was a fenced yard (fence already falling down), we could find no trace of an orchard or garden.

We wondered what had happened to the family and surmised that they had become victims of the influenza epidemic of the year of 1918. We thought that may have been the reason because people at that time would have been afraid of going to the home of people who had died from it. We also thought that the reason there had been no vandalism was because the place was so out-of-the-way. Of course at that time that would have not been a problem like today. As it looked, I suppose we were about as near to vandalism as there was in those days by just exploring. We decided we would go back there some day but those thoughts left as we had no business there in the first place.

Visiting Coal Mines

WHEN THE STOCKMANS and the Mertens and the Veits came to visit us in Columbia I would take them to the Lindberg coal mine and let them ride the huge dragline used for removing the overburden of 70 feet of dirt. This thing was three stories tall with a 450-horsepower diesel engine that powered the winches to scoop the dirt. The second story had a 350-horsepower engine that handled the electric generator for operating the outfit and also furnished the lights for the 24-hour day of work.

Dragline excavator

The thing sat on a round base of solid steel 40 feet in diameter. It had two 24-foot-long paddles, shaped like those of a row boat. When a paddle contacted the ground, it raised that side of the machine eight inches and rolled the base on the dirt on the other side. It waddled like a duck and moved forward 18 inches at a time. The boom on the thing was 300 feet long and had an 18-yard scoop on the end, and even when the scoop was full of dirt the machine was heavy enough that it would not tip over.

A cable was attached to the scoop with a huge chain that was hooked to each side of the scoop with the cable attached to the center. Believe this, the chain was so heavy that after it was worn out a man was not strong enough to pick up three links from the ground.

The beautiful part about this was that you could spend the whole afternoon riding the machine with the operator, watching it work.

They hauled the coal with three huge tractor trucks pulling fifth-wheel trailers that hauled 40 tons at a trip. It was raining one Sunday while we were there and as the trucks came up that 70-foot incline they would spin out. They would not climb that grade that rainy day and just sat there spinning their tires until a D-8 "cat" would run up behind and help it up the climb. It was odd that with eight huge tires on the truck, the trailer had only two huge tires on the rear. Be assured those tires were furnished by General Tire Company, not in my territory but by field man partner Eddy Marriot. This was a great deal for him because we worked for that 10% commission and one of those rear trailer tires cost that coal company a little over $3,000 then and weighed over a ton and a half.

I had coal mines in my territory and one was at Bevier, Missouri but it was not a dragline like at Lindberg. Since it had only 24 feet of overburden, they used a huge shovel. The thing was self-leveling with two tracks on each corner, like a Caterpillar tractor, that were 12 feet long with a track on each side of the huge shafts, two of which could turn to guide the thing. It was very quiet in operation. This company was serviced by Firestone and I just could not change them over as neither could my predecessor Byrul Smarr. Although we could visit there, we could not ride the machine.

Bevier, Missouri coal mine

The little coal mine that I had hauled from in my coal business days was in my territory. This mine followed a creek valley and went through timber, but they did not cut any trees. It was a dragline operation because of the depth of the dirt and had only a small scoop of eight yards. The operator would swing up to a large tree and stop the scoop real fast and the darn thing would swing out on the cable and he would beat those trees into pieces and keep digging through the stumps. I would say this mine was somewhat on the "two-bit" side.

Traveling Salesman

GENERAL TIRE was a family-owned company. They had five commission warehouses that took care of the state of Missouri. The tires were shipped to these warehouses, which were contracted to an individual. The individual handled the selling end, paying the company for the tires sold, and as the sales slips went to the company, the tires were replaced by that inventory. At Columbia the contractor was Whitely Oil Company.

Eddy Marriot was the field man for the northeast part of Missouri. His boundary was from Columbia along U.S. Highway 63 to the Missouri River, then east along it to Missouri Highway 19, then north on Highway 19 to U.S. 54 and along it to the Mississippi river, then north to the Iowa line and all the territory of small towns east of U.S. 63 south back to Columbia. He, like I, had two nights away from home, spending his one-day route including the clay mining area around Mexico, Missouri to Centralia.

My route was more far-reaching. I left Columbia on U.S. 40 (now I-70) heading for Booneville and crossed the river there, followed U.S. 40 to Marshall, Missouri, crossing the river again at Waverly on U.S. 65, and stayed overnight in Chillicothe, Missouri. That day I would weave back and forth between U.S. 24 and the Missouri River. I left Columbia on Monday morning. On Tuesday morning I worked the area between U.S. 36 south to U.S. 24 east to U.S. 63 and came back home that evening. The idea was to work trucking companies, service stations, garages, and implement companies for farm tires.

General Tire had a plan where you would go to a town or a country service station and sell them tires at dealer's cost and their profit was whatever they could get above that. You especially hunted for a good dealer and gave him this kind of deal. He was supposed to work the truckers but we did that for him. In this way we could sign a contract through him for the trucker who had to buy a minimum of $1,200 worth of tires every 12 months. If you could sell such a contract, General Tire would give them a sub-dealer deal of 10% below dealer cost. Half of this 10% would go to the trucker and that would give the service station (or dealer) 5% below his dealer cost and on all tires he would not have to be responsible for collecting the money from the trucker. He was responsible for the collection on his other tires sold. This made the tire cheaper for the trucker and also gave the dealer a small chance of undercutting another dealer of a different brand. It went over well. You have to remember that in those days of gravel roads, tires did not give the service they do today. We worked like heck with these truckers because they were where the money was on commission sales for us.

On Wednesday I had a one-day route that covered south of the Missouri River east of U.S. 65 between the river and Highway 50, then south on Missouri Highway 5 to U.S. Route 66 (now I-44) to Waynesville (Ft. Leonard Wood), then Missouri Highway 17 to Iberia, to Crocker, to St. Elizabeth, to Meta, to St. Thomas, and then to Jefferson City and back home. I had to stay clear of the Jefferson City store where I started working. I can tell you this, I sold more tires in the Jefferson City area than did that store. The company told me to go ahead because if I could sell tires there it was because the store was not doing its job. So I got John Groner Transport and Transport Delivery of Tulsa, Oklahoma. I made it my business to hit Jefferson City just when drivers were getting back from their deliveries. Sometimes I worked until 10 o'clock at night. The work was physical. The truck I drove was equipped with a V-8 Ford engine, which ran on four cylinders with the other four being equipped as an air compressor. The truck, a one and a half ton, carried the new tires I had sold or the ones I had recapped for the truckers. It was part of my job to manhandle these big tires, installing them on the truck rims after removing the ones to be replaced. Believe me, this was hard work.

On Thursday I again headed for Jefferson City and took Highway 50 to Linn, then to Missouri Highway 89 and on it to Chamois and then down Missouri Highway 100 to Missouri Highway 19. It was in the Morrison area where I ran into the Mertens family of my grandfather's brother. Seems like these Mertens were money men as two were bankers. I learned that, as we went to local bankers for credit references. Did a little talking there too. One of them was a hospital administrator, as I will tell you about when I get to my daughter Karen being born.

I followed Missouri Highway 100 to Herman, Missouri, then on Missouri Highway 19 to Highway 50 to Rosebud, Missouri. From Rosebud I used Missouri Highway 28 to Owensville and it was here I stayed overnight.

It was in Rosebud that I ran into my first deadbeat. His name was Wehmeyer and he ran the Ford dealership there and also had 10 Ford F-8 clay trucks. The banker warned me to be careful in accepting any of his checks. Well, our warehouse manager, I.L. Davis, thought it necessary to check up on the quality of service we field men were giving. So he met me one morning and rode with me while I was working Owensville. While we were there, someone told him about the Rosebud Ford dealer and his 10 trucks. Of course I.L. thought we should call upon this man. We did, and after I.L. introduced us, Mr. Wehmeyer said, "General Tire? I always wanted to be their dealer," and he promptly ordered $900 worth of tires. He said, "When you deliver them, just present the invoice to my cashier" (who worked in a cage like in a bank in those days).

On our way to Owensville I got a talking-to about how I had missed such a good customer. When I went to pick up the check after those tires were delivered, I received the check just as promised but wouldn't you know it, the darn thing bounced. Of course it was my responsibility to collect. The next week I went to them about the check bouncing and received a big spiel about how that could not be; just run it again and, as it turned out, again and again.

Finally the Big Boss came to me and said, "We will change our tactics. Go to the bank in Owensville each evening and again the next morning and one of these days we will catch him after he makes a deposit." I carried that $900 check for eight months before collecting. Each day the banker would just come back shaking his head. After I cashed the check, I had to carry the money with me and I purchased a billfold with a chain to my belt. When I got back I gave that damn money to I.L. and told him to, from now on, keep his nose out of my business. By the way that Wehmeyer dealership was still there the last time we drove up Highway 50 to St. Louis.

I had some trouble with I.L. even before all this. We had a unique printing cash register (no computer type in those days) and only five of us had a key to operate it. This was because all invoices had to be sent to headquarters for inventory replacement. Each operator had a number and it was used along with the invoice number, cash or charge, and each voided ticket turned in also. In this way the company could figure our commission and "jack us up" on "behind" unpaid invoices. We were also bonded, so if there was any variance between warehouse inventory and sales inventory the shortage was among the five who had a key to the register.

Eddy came up short some 10 by 20 truck tires and after much investigating by the bonding company it was decided they were either lost or stolen. We got a stern talk from the bonding company about how the next time it would be taken out of our skin. We were then required to lock all tires to be delivered and were furnished with the necessary locks and chains to do so. This was not a bad idea, especially since we had the overnight stay in a hotel.

Well, one day the cash register was found open and came up $20 short and in checking, my key number was found to be the culprit. After checking this out, the only possibility I could figure was that because I kept my key on a key chain and, another key from my chain could have extended down into the money drawer and kept it from latching. I lucked out on this, as the morning after the shortage was discovered, a professor from the University of Missouri came in early when I was in the office and handed me a $20 bill and said, "Give this to I.L. He gave me too much change back from the set of new tires I bought." Did it ever do me good to hand I.L. that $20! This should have learned him not to accuse but that still did not stop him from doing it. You can bet I darn sure watched my business after that.

Fun Day with Quentin

IN OWENSVILLE I had a great customer, Brinkman Transfer. This business converted to clay haulers under contract to General Chemical Company to haul all of their clay. To do this required 38 trucks.

General Chemical Company is still there today, on the short end of the Rock Island Railroad tracks still being used. They and the MFA Feed Plant in Union, Missouri are why Southern Pacific keeps the tracks. The rest of the Rock Island line is abandoned and Southern Pacific has track rights on Union Pacific and here in California, Missouri we can hardly get across the tracks between trains. Go see this General Chemical plant sometime. It is a long tube about eight feet in diameter and 100 feet long that turns slowly and lays on a slant. They dump the clay into the top and, after being burned with intense heat, it comes out the lower end as a fine powder, which was at that time used as a base for face powder for women. The heat could be changed and that was used to make the insulation for spark plugs for car motors. This thing burned five railroad cars of #5 fuel oil every 24 hours. This type of oil was almost crude and had to be heated to get it out of the cars and to the burners.

After my overnight stay in Owensville, and working the many clay haulers, I headed for Bland, Belle, Vichy, and Rolla, then headed back to Vienna, then Freeburg and here had another trucker, Ben Berhorst. (He was the man who loaned the money to Mr. Luebbert who gave us our trouble when building our new home those years before.) It was back to home those Friday evenings and the completion of my week's work. I had to work every other Saturday, splitting with Eddy Marriot.

We worked the truckers out of Columbia and Mexico. This was mostly the Wetterau Grocery chain and they are still operating, only now out of St. Louis.

This was the route where Quentin and I had our day of "fun." That surely must have been the day after a holiday as I cannot figure why I would have had to make it a one-day trip otherwise. On that day the roads were covered with ice because of freezing rain the night before. The highway department did not even put cinders on Highway 50 then. Nevertheless I sped along at about 50 miles an hour with that truck on the ice until we came upon a highway patrol car with its rear wheels hung up on the right shoulder, crossways in the highway with the front blocking our lane. I slowed down and swung around the patrol car, stopping on the right shoulder. We both got out to help the patrolman and as I stepped out of the truck I fell down on the ice and slid all the way across the highway. This convinced me that the road was slick and after rescuing the patrolman I drove at a more sedate speed of about 30 miles an hour. We weren't sure if we would make it up the Linn hill at that speed but we did.

This was an ill-fated trip in a number of ways. We changed the rear tires on a school bus at Owensville and had a little trouble with the air hose wanting to freeze up as we inflated the tires. Then to top it all off, we forgot the jack under the bus and drove close to 15 miles before we remembered it and had to drive back over that ice to get it. Things then went smoothly until we reached Wardsville where we changed tires on Vincent Schrimpf's milk truck. By this time it was around 10 o'clock at night, the temperature had dropped to 10 degrees above zero, and our air hose kept freezing up. When it did, we would disconnect it and take it in the house where Vi Schrimpf let us thaw it out in her oven. After doing this a number of times we finally finished and headed back to Columbia and got home around midnight. There we got the scolding of our lives from Ida because we had forgotten to tell her Quentin was going to play hooky from school and go along with me. Sheesh, what a day!

Karen is Born

WELL I HAVE REACHED THE FIFTIES in my story so I'll go on to 1951. Ted was born two years and five months after Dave so we were very surprised when Ida learned she was pregnant although nursing Ted. She had to wean him immediately, as the doctor found her to be anemic. He had her eating lots and lots of liver to correct the iron deficiency and that later caused a problem when our daughter was born.

We still had our boarders. Earl got rid of his old Chevy and came up with Elmer Jr.'s 1939 Dodge Coupe.

Missouri River flooding at Walnut and McCarty Street, Jefferson City, 1951 [4]

The year 1951 was the year of the great Missouri River flood, where concrete highways were washed away and railroad track was twisted and destroyed by the force of the water, and that caught Ida and me with her mom and dad while on vacation. Believe this, we drove all the way to Hermann to get back to Columbia, since the bridge crossing the Missouri at Jefferson City and the connecting highways U.S. 63 and U.S. 54 were covered by high water. When we got there that Sunday evening, we found the front door standing open. When Earl had left for home that Friday evening he didn't get the front door latched. We supposed that the wind had blown it open. Those were the days when one did not have to worry about theft and we found nothing missing. Thank God it was summer or we would have had a nice heat bill. Back in late 1950 the same developer who built our subdivision developed another just across Broadway and our neighbors, Richard and Tish Jackson, purchased a new larger home there and suggested that we do also. They sold their old home to a man buying rental property and our new neighbor became John Carroll and family. He and Quentin both studied electrical engineering at the University of Missouri and the two of them used to cram together for exams. After Quentin and John graduated, John took a position with a radio station at Boulder, Colorado. John later advanced to a high position with the Federal Communications Commission and was with the government when we last heard from him. We wrote to each other and about seven years ago learned that his wife, LaVerne, had died from cancer. We have not heard from John since that letter.

On October 7, 1951 Karen was born, just one year, five months and 27 days after Ted. It was here that we received quite a scare that I will always remember. After she was born, she was brought to me and I noted that she was very blue. Emil and Cath had come up to visit with us that Sunday and someone told them that we were at the hospital so they dropped by. I remember that well, as they were with me when the nurse showed Karen to us. I commented to the nurse that she looked really blue and she said it would change when she was cleaned up. After a while the three of us had a visit with Ida and it was about two o'clock and since Ida was tired we left. She told me to go to Jefferson City to tell Mom and Dad about the baby and to stay for supper with them and to stop in at the hospital on the way back. When I got back I learned they had been trying to contact me because they thought the baby was a "blue baby" (a hole in her heart chamber) and had placed her in an incubator. We cried together but God was again with us as, after many tests, they discovered that by Ida eating all that liver the iron was going into the baby's system. Ida stayed with her to nurse her and she did clear and we were so thankful.

Baby Karen

For many years on her birthday her brothers told her she could not have a birthday celebration because she was hatched. She could not understand what they were talking about and Ida and I had to stomp on those two to get them to stop. That was the end of the incubator thing and being hatched instead of being born.

I told you I would get to the Mertens from Morrison when I got to Karen's birth. This came about because I had company insurance when Karen was born (she was the only one). We had no insurance before that. This policy paid for Ida and was supposed to cover the baby if it lived one hour after birth. They refused to pay and I was called about it by the hospital administrator who was a Mertens. She was born and raised in Morrison. When she learned I was a Mertens clan member she stated, "I will do everything I can to get the insurance to pay," but each time she sent it in they would deny the claim. After all her effort it still fell to us to pay the additional cost of Karen's hospital stay and that cut our savings short.

Some Sad, Some Hard, and Some Amusing Things about Life in Columbia

CATHOLICS WERE A MINORITY in Columbia although it was a university town. We became members of Sacred Heart Parish. Father Flood was our pastor and he alone made up for any hardships of living in Columbia. The assistant was a redhead and a pretty tough cookie to go to confession to. So it ended up that Father Flood heard confessions while this guy just sat in his confessional. I suppose he just twiddled his thumbs. Maybe he was actually smart since he had gotten out of the "work."

The amusing thing was the antics of the girls at Stephens College, an all-girls Baptist school that was just across the street from Sacred Heart. Sacred Heart was three stories tall and Stephens College was two stories and the girls would sunbathe in the nude on the roof of that building. The Sister who was principal at Sacred Heart was concerned that the eighth-grade boys could look out the window and see the girls and those boys sure did much looking. Sister came to Father Flood for a solution to such goings on and the two of them decided to paint the window panes black so the boys could not look out at the girls. To tease, the girls took pictures of the black windows and then took those pictures to the Columbia Tribune newspaper and began a contest as to who could identify the mystery windows of Columbia, Missouri. Well! It didn't take long to become quite an uproar and an embarrassment to our church.

The hard thing came about for almost the same reason. Just across the street west from our church, the Methodist church had a large student union building and began inviting the 3,000 Catholic students to join in all the things we Catholics couldn't do and to proselytize the Catholics attending the University of Missouri (or so they thought). I had joined the Knights of Columbus of Sacred Heart Council on November 11, 1949 and thereby was available to become a member of a committee to do something about this.

After many meetings with the Catholic students (those who would attend) we decided we would build a building for our youth that would be in competition. In survey after survey, we came up with this solution and it was acted on. Of the 3,000 Catholic students, they thought half could not afford to make any donation. That left 1,500 students and of these it was thought that 750 wouldn't donate even if they could afford to, so we asked the entire student body to put $1 into an envelope every third month hoping that the 750 that could would do so. The people pledged the amount for the building and each of the parish members were assessed the amount above what was to be gotten from the students.

We received a piddly $39 the first collection. That amount became less as time passed. We then had to go back to the people for another pledge and that became "hellfire and damnation" on their part. I will never get into such an idea again. Ida and I were still paying on our pledge two years after we moved away from Columbia.

Deciding to Become Farmers

JUST BEFORE CHRISTMAS OF 1951 something shocking happened. Our neighbors hired a 13-year-old girl as their babysitter so they could attend a Christmas party. They had two little boys about the ages of our two. When they arrived home from the party, they found the babysitter had been raped and strangled to death with the floor lamp cord. The two boys were asleep and not harmed. A police dog tracked the man right behind our home and that scared us too. The man was never caught. The distraught family sold their home and moved out of the state.

On January 1 General Tire came up with a new idea that both Eddy and I did not appreciate. I suppose we were making too much money with the 10% commission. They reduced it to 5% and increased the guaranteed pay from $250 per month to $350. This meant a cut in pay. Also my area contained Montgomery Ward and their new man, Frank Seaver, would undercut any contract I had with a trucker, especially south of the Missouri River. It was said that the Jefferson City store would use the sales of their other products and lose money on tires until they put General Tire out of business. Of course that meant me too.

This cut me from over $5,200 per year to about $4,500 or less. I was told that I would just have to work harder and I felt I was already working to my limit. This sort of thing takes much of the initiative away from a person and you then get the attitude of what's the use. In a way it told me that I had already reached the limit of further advancement. Maybe I can be called a job jumper but I thought it was time to move on. Eddy stayed with the job. Maybe he was a better salesman.

Since Ida did not like the idea of being alone, especially after the rape and murder, after much debating, we decided to become farmers. I suppose that came from both of us being raised on a farm. We knew that we could not instantly become farmers so we kept mum to the boss and began looking.

Two things helped in this regard. One was that I was servicing the lime haulers here at California and was asked by Mr. Lawson to come back to the old job of lime hauling, so I knew I could get a job there. The second was Emil's brother-in-law, Joe Nilges (the fellow I borrowed the shirt from to get married.) He was a good tire customer of mine at Linn, Missouri and was also the GMC truck and Pontiac dealer there so I could get a good deal on a GMC truck and lime bed. The only problem was that after paying the hospital bill for Karen we were short of money and money was necessary for the change and for security.

There is one thing I have to say about my wife Ida: she agreed to every change I felt we were in need of. The only thing she did not want to do was to move to town when we retired. So it was that when we made our decision, she was willing to move into a farm home that we rented that was not modern.

Now we come back to the John Carroll family. Since they were renting from the man who purchased the Jackson home, we obtained his address from them and offered to sell him our home. We got enough profit from that sale so that we had free rent for those years. The equity amounted to the figure needed for the down payment on the truck and lime bed. We had truck payments of $138 per month and the rent payment of $25 per month. We rented the vacant home of the old County Agent Victor Gray's second farm he purchased. It was a small home and we lived there while looking at farms to buy. When the John Carroll family learned we had sold the home in Columbia, they rented it and moved into it as we moved out. We had the backyard fenced and had a swing set and teeter-totter in it. They had three daughters and the backyard was just what they wanted. Both families made that move on the July 4, 1952.

On June 1 of 1952 I gave notice to I.L. Davis (my manager) that I was leaving, giving him the month to find my replacement. He said he was not worried as he knew I would not quit such a good job. He never found (and I don't think tried to find) my replacement and on my final week I took my friend Dave Morris with me so he could get to know the route. I never asked I.L. and it was then he realized that Ida and I were leaving Columbia. I thought maybe Dave would take the position but after the week he said no way. What a relief to be rid of that job and be with my family for the entire week. And to that farm home that was not modern and it was back to the outhouse for a while. But at least I no longer had the worry of collecting past due accounts, of being at lawsuits as a witness when an account had to be sued, or the responsibility of carrying company money under bond. I never realized the stress of that job until I experienced the freedom of life after I left.

Moving to the Country

SO IT WAS to the little farm home and to the country for the kids.

David on toy tractor, Ted in wagon

Since there was a poultry house, we decided to have chickens. It was late for chickens but still time enough to grow fryers and we purchased 200 of the things. The idea was to save some hens for layers and eggs but most of the darn chickens were roosters. We began to eat them when they were still small. As they grew bigger we knew we had to do something so Ida contacted her sister-in-law Gerri and asked if she and Willard would like some fryers cheap. Of course they would. So the two dressed the darn roosters and we placed our share in the locker plant here that was owned by the Boss Lawson's sons. (They knew by this time about freezer wrapping paper).

We had always liked fried chicken but by the time we got all of those chickens eaten I added chicken to my list of things I was sick of from having too much, like ice cream and picture shows that summer when I stayed with Clarence and Anna. I could understand then why Clarence did not like to eat chicken either. His dislike lasted longer than mine.

Me and Ida

Another thing, I found time on my hands although we had a garden. So I made a doll bed out of dynamite boxes for Karen and a rocking chair for myself out of an old hog pen. I found an old drill like Dad had with two cranks for large drills for mortise work in the building of large barns and after cleaning it up I gave it to Clarence. I wonder if that thing is still sitting around the Veit farm someplace.

At Christmas, after getting the Christmas tree, we found it was too large so we cut off the bottom end. I made two end-table lamps from it for Ida. When moving here to town when we retired, we lost one (as well as our alarm clock) and we still have the other one. The rocking chair accompanied all the kids to college (nearly got burned somewhere.) I have it in our basement here now by a reading light and, to brag on myself, will say it is the most comfortable chair ever although somewhat narrow. Must have been skinny in those days.

Working on Houses

IN THE EARLY WINTER AND SPRING Emil, his son Donald, Evy, and I took the job of rebuilding the large old white house Elmer and Rose bought just across Dunklin Street, converting it into a five-apartment house by enlarging it.

Remember when I told you about getting out of the Army and helping Emil brick his house? We thought we could do anything and we did because money was always a necessity and I've often wondered why.

So we took on one of the dirtiest damn jobs ever in that old house. Even all the other people thought so. Part of the dirt was due to the fact that the house had at one time been on fire and charred wood from that fire was still in some parts of the house. We knocked off all the old plaster and laths and shoveled all the crap out the window. That old house was level with Dunklin but the backside was level to an alley between Dunklin and Elm. We just threw all the crap out the window; that is, until the police arrived. Someone had complained about the dust and thereafter we had to carry it all down three flights of stairs with buckets and empty the buckets easy like. It was then that I began to have doubts about being a carpenter. We got that apartment finished by working our a---s off. If you ever worked with Emil that was exactly what it amounted to. Should have joined a union.

Next was plastering Maggie Siebeneck's house. For God's sake. Someone came up with a wire mesh to replace plaster laths. Emil and Evy were the plasterers and old Bud the mud-mixer and those darn guys pushed all the mud right through that wire. With all the mud mixing I had to do, I think every stud in that house is filled in between with plaster. That just has to be a solid house.

Then it came the Rademan house and here we had sheet rock to plaster over and was that lovely. Here I could sit on my butt sometimes.

After that job it was on to Herb Huhmann for a plaster job and this was upgraded to sand finish. Well you can learn and we did. We learned to forget a little corner in one bedroom. To do sand finish you put the finish on and when it began to set, you went back with a sponge and sponged the sand out for the sand finish. You will not believe this—we forgot about a 10-minute job just at quitting time. When we got back the next morning this spot had already set so hard nothing could be done about it but accept our boss Red's chewing out. We had hoped he wouldn't notice it, but remember, Red Ben Adrian is our kin and our kin notices everything.

Oh! For the love of lime hauling and to get back to it.

Buying a Farm

IN 1953 WE PURCHASED OUR SECOND NEW CAR because we wanted a sedan and to get away from the 1950 two-door. It had overdrive and was the car used to go to Uncle Gus's funeral in Cunningham, Kansas. Twenty-six miles to the gallon and at 70 miles per hour.

In the fall of 1953 Dave began school and it was to the little one-room school. The school had already been consolidated into the California R-1 district but, not having room, they used all the small one-rooms the first year. From then on, the schools were supposed to produce smarter kids and I believe today that consolidating was a mistake, because it was the start of expensive schooling.

The next spring we found an 80-acre farm that we could afford because it was well run down and the home had not been lived in for the past eight years. The house was unpainted and Ed Imhoff and Ida's dad both thought we were crazy to buy such. Our answer to that was it was the only place we found cheap enough that we had enough savings for the down payment. We purchased it from a man by the name of Floyd Cliburn who lived as a bachelor with his mother. The asking price was $6,000 and our counter offer was $5,000. After a while he made us the price of $5,500.

On the farm was an old flat-head, two-cylinder John Deere like I had never seen before with a rigid beam two-bottom, 14-inch plow and both had been unused for several years. It was on steel wheels and reminded me of a small threshing machine tractor. We told Floyd Cliburn that if he would throw in the tractor, he had a deal. He did, and Evy and Emil came up with their families one Sunday and we decided to start the thing and surprisingly it started right up. I thought that I now also had a tractor to farm with.

Mr. Cliburn did not know it but we had the farm appraised by the Tipton Farmer's Bank and they said the buildings alone were worth his asking price so it was through that bank that we financed the balance. I had gone back to the Tipton bank because they knew me from my years before and that decision paid off. We moved to the home, again on July 4, in the year of 1954.

Well that old tractor gave me several scares. One was when that fall I thought I should sow a field of wheat and of course to do that one had to first plow the land. It took a brick to clean all the rust off the plow moldboards and I was ready. The field I intended to plow had spots of sheet erosion and more of Buffalo grass which was tough to plow.

I don't know the year of that John Deere's birth but it must have been in the early 1920s since it was a valve-in-block motor and the only John Deere I ever saw with such a motor. It only had two speeds forward. Low was slow and high was fast and reverse was just as fast as high and this gave me the surprise of my life. I was popping up a slight grade and the old tractor was really talking. Well, the shift pattern of that ancient tractor transmission was that low was straight across from reverse. On the hard pull, the transmission flew out of low, right into reverse. All of a sudden I was backing up real fast until the rigid beam plow's back landslide caught in the dirt and raised one rear wheel up in the air almost turning over and I darn near dirtied my pants. I'd been stomping my left foot looking for the clutch, only to remember that the darn thing had a hand clutch. I then had to rig me a deal where I could tie the shift lever in low because of that darn cross-shift.

Well I thought I had the problem solved until I got it in a really hard pull and with the shift lever tied in low the clutch would jump out. With the hand clutch I could sit in the seat and hold the clutch lever in with my foot. Each time we went uphill I would rear back in the seat firmly grasping the steering for support and we would manage to get up the hill. Of course that seat extended so far back that you sat over the implement instead of the tractor.

Next I needed a disc and that was two worn-out tandem discs from the Henry Tractor Company. One had a good front and the other had a good rear so I put the two good together and had a fair tandem disc and a hell of a lot of leftover parts for replacement.

Tandem disc

Then I needed a wheat drill.

Wheat drill

I saw one for sale on a public sale so I went to look it over and thought it was worth $75. It had steel wheels and rubber tires. So I sent Ida to do the buying on sale day and she bought the thing after being told the wheels belonged to his side delivery rake and would be replaced with the original ones. She became angry with the guy bidding against her and "showed" him she was not going to back down. (I sometimes think it was the owner bidding against her.) She ran the bidding up to $90 and the owner was so happy he delivered it for free with the wooden wheels and one of those had spokes broken out.

We got the wheat sowed that fall with the drill and its wobbling wheel. One thing about Ida. She is determined and doesn't give up. Her comment was, "He made me so mad that I showed him I would get it." Thank God he gave up at $90. I'll admit I kept my mouth shut. Yet that old drill, with some steel rim wheels I found for it, sowed several crops of wheat and oats before we traded it in on a new Case. The old wooden wheels were placed on each side of the mail box post for a reminder to Ida and a decoration.

One thing to note. Since I was hauling lime you have to remember that most of the work I am speaking of was done just before or after dark.

Making the Farm Livable

THIS WAS ALL TAKING PLACE in the fall of 1954 and just before fall we almost lost our son Ted. Not too long after we moved to the farm he became sick. Ida took him to Dr. Latham at Latham Hospital and his diagnosis was the stomach flu, as that was going around at the time. But Ted seemed to be getting sicker so Ida took him to the doctor again. Since Ted was just over four years old and not vomiting, the doctor did not even consider appendicitis. So he sent Ida home with some medicine. When I thought about myself having appendicitis, I remembered vomiting along with diarrhea. She went back again.

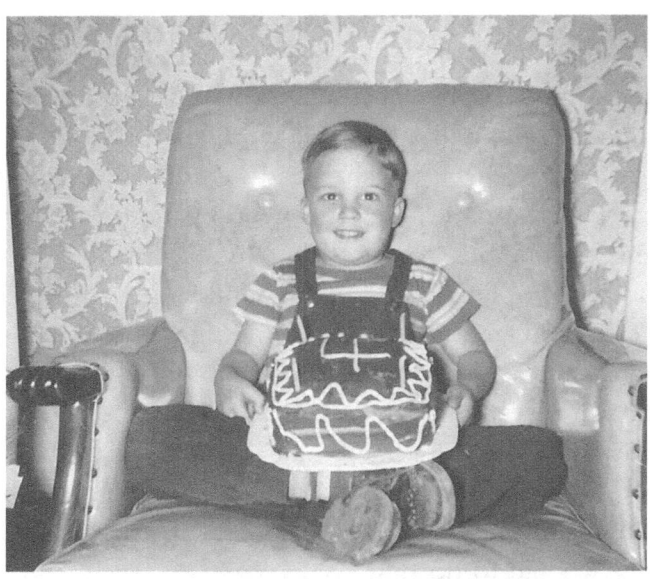

Ted, four years old

At that time a young doctor (a World War II veteran) had joined Dr. Latham and this time Ida got him. She told him our concern and, thank God, he took a blood sample and noted the high white cell count. He would not let her take Ted home and instead rushed him to surgery. The appendix had already ruptured and be assured we had one sick little boy on our hands.

Ida and I had to stay with him for eight days (I at night and she at day) but he finally began to respond and it was then that we knew he had passed the crisis. I will never forget how bad he wanted a drink of water but could have none. The doctor said to let him suck a damp washcloth to wet his mouth. The poor little guy completely rubbed the skin off the end of his nose just wiping his mouth. We were relieved when they finally removed the drain and let us take him home. From that time on we were more persistent when taking a child to a doctor and not just accepting his word.

To give you an idea of the costs in those days, the total bill for the hospital stay and the three doctors was only $191.

The home we moved into had not been lived in for eight years because, as we learned later, the man we purchased it from had a mental health issue and was in and out of the mental hospital. He had started to remodel it and had put in a new kitchen ceiling of acoustic tile and lowered the ceiling. The person who put the cabinets in surely had never seen any before because they were more like closets. He failed to put in a countertop with a space between the top cabinets and the bottom ones, although he did extend the lower cabinet out. They just did not have a work space. Strange.

There were two back porches and he had converted the north one into a bathroom, leaving the window that was between the kitchen and porch, but painting the thing white for privacy. The bathroom was completed and a septic tank had been placed in along with the sewer and laterals. All the plumbing was in the house as was a sink under the east window in those cabinet-closets. He just had not got the water system in and that was because he had to dig under the foundation of the house. We had to leave it like that, using the outhouse during the day and carrying two five-gallon buckets of water for nighttime use. It was not too far to the well. There were other things we had to do first.

One was that we wanted to send David to Catholic school. In the fall of 1954 we tried to get the church to get a school bus but they would not. So 10 families purchased the old Booneville Auto Parts one-ton panel truck and drove it 37 miles twice a day to get our kids a Catholic education, with Ida being the driver. This old panel truck, converted to a bus by placing a board along each side for seats and painted yellow, got our church one priest and one nun. Then too many families wanted their kids hauled, so we purchased a 1947 along with the old 1946 and increased our Catholic attendance to 113 pupils from the 37 before. We incorporated as the McGirk Bus Company and later gave both buses to the church. Both wore out so our new pastor Father Owens bought a 1958 GMC and a used 1957 Chevrolet.

Panel truck school bus

Driving that old bus must have shaken something loose in Ida as she was surprised to learn she was pregnant again. After three years and nine months we had given up hope of another child. Beverly was born at the Latham Hospital attended by the young doctor who had saved Ted. This was Dr. Lionel Gallagher and he remained our doctor until he was killed in an automobile accident. Beverly's birth date was July 9, 1955.

Baby Beverly

When Ida was quilting the other day she and the other women began talking about the olden days, including when Ida was driving the school bus. Gertrude Leonard (whose children rode the bus) told Ida, "When you were driving that old school bus and you were expecting, I just knew it had to be a girl." Ida asked her how she knew. Her reply was, "That old bus shook the b---s off a boy so it had to be a girl." Now don't tell me women do not talk together as men do. Shame on us all.

We just never took time to sit down. I dug the hole under the house for the water line. I took up the old well pump and put in a two-stage jet in the storm cellar that was outside of the house. I got the pump and plastic pipe from Scruggs-Guhlman, who at that time also had a lumber yard at Centertown. I put that water system in and immediately the pipes began splitting and I was given new pipe to replace the bad ones, doing all the digging again. Ida placed her washing machine in the cellar where we had also put the hot water heater and upon draining it found the cellar drain stopped up. I dug down trying to find where the drain was clogged only to learn that when the home was built in 1912 they just put the pipe through the cellar wall and stopped there. Well, that meant more digging, and deep through the hardest hardpan (a mixture of gravel and clay about as hard as concrete) ever. It took me a couple of months and of course it was done of an evening.

In the meantime, Karen fell into the open trench and broke her arm. She complained, but we pushed it off as a sprain and went to a free picture show at Centertown. Those were still being put on by stores in small towns, shown against a building wall after dark. Since they were free we went. We bought the kids a Coke and Karen in trying to hold hers said it hurt so we took her to the doctor the next day and learned her arm was broken. He put a splint on it so she now had a weapon to learn her older brothers some sense.

David, Beverly, Karen, Ted, circa 1956

Once we got the water system in, we gave our outhouse to Roger Mertens and J.B DeWesplore (both brothers-in-law) for their crapper house at a clubhouse they had on the Osage River. They backed their truck up to it and with much effort we got it pushed on the truck. Well! The bottom was not the prettiest thing you ever saw and as they drove down the road those two holes looked just like eyes and "looked" right at everyone who was following. Whatever did they think?

Hauling the old outhouse [5]

The next thing we did was install storm windows and we had that done by our nephew Elmer Stockman Jr. because I could work later in his remodeling work to pay off the bill. At that time he was in the business of making a new kind of storm window.

We brought a fuel oil heating stove with us from the Gray home we had been renting and it was a good one. We got it from Scheidt's Hardware and Bottle business along with a Magic Chef gas stove. They were so happy with the deal that they gave Ida a Salad Master and it was all chrome and is still in use today. We needed another stove, which we purchased from them, and that stove almost burned the house down. Those things had a carburetor and if they ran out of fuel it took time to get the fuel to the fire pot. Ida filled the tank and forgot to light it. When she thought about it, it had about one inch of raw fuel in it. She took a spoon and dipped out as much as she could, put in a bunch of old rags to dry it out, and did not relight it until I got home. We did the chores and she told me about it and I looked it over but saw nothing to keep me from lighting it. We were eating supper when we heard a rumble in the living room and found the heater dancing on the floor.

I ran out to the school bus and got the fire extinguisher and could knock the fire down but it would just explode right back again. We put salt in it and that seemed to help. We called the neighbors thinking we could use gunny sacks to carry it out since it was a cabinet style stove with the fire box enclosed. By that time the inside was red hot, as was the stove pipe. Our neighbor, who had just butchered, brought over his excess salt and after filling the firebox with salt got it extinguished.

It seems that many times we were chosen to compromise. One such time was when Scheidt's Gas, who was furnishing our heating gas, came to me with a proposition of going to a 1,000-gallon propane tank. They had a monthly filling system and in our operation we used more than 500 gallons a month so that required an extra trip at times. They asked if we would purchase a tank they were removing from Holt Summit since that city had received natural gas. Gas cost us $.11 per gallon and with a 1,000-gallon tank it would be $.10 and they then could service all with a monthly or bi-monthly trip. To do so they would trade in our 500-gallon tank and make us a good deal on the used 1,000-gallon and the trade-in difference of $250. Were we surprised that this tank was 60% full and they just gave that gas to us as it was already given to them so we received the tank at a $190 cost and it is still on the farm today. We learned if you do another a favor, you will often receive one in return.

This takes us up to December 20, 1955 when I began the 39th year of my life. Ida was 31.

Early Dairy Days

Growing Wheat and Milking Cows

AS I BEGIN THIS CHAPTER the date is May 22, 1993 and as you read along you will say to yourself, "These two people must not have been of right mind" and we will agree to that. It may be that we were determined, poor, and with enough guts to give a try for success in life. I will add that all the crazy things paid off in the long run. So I will begin this chapter regardless of what you think.

David's first communion

In the spring, David made his First Communion and that summer his sister was born.

That summer also saw us with a wheat crop to harvest and no way to bind the grain, so we cut it for hay. The year 1955 was the last year of threshing in our area and the machine was owned by the Baumgartner brothers. I helped Bruce Cook and Herman Kirchhoff with their threshing and they in turn had helped me put up my wheat crop for hay about a month before. The year we purchased the farm one of the quarry workers put up the hay crop that was late but still worth cutting and did so for one-half.

We still had the old steel-wheeled John Deere tractor but no mower so we purchased an old horse-drawn McCormick-Deering mower from Ida's dad. He had cut the wheels down and put on rims and rubber tires. He also cut off the tongue and made a tractor hitch. We gave him $15 for it and it, along with a foolish man and woman, got the wheat cut. I say foolish because Ida rode that mower cutting the crop just a month and a half before Beverly was born. She refused to drive the old tractor. She probably had the easier riding because of the rubber tires.

Now Ida put a little canvas car seat in that old bus, stuck Bev's legs through the holes, and tied her in and that baby, along with Karen and Ted, rode that old bus over 80 miles a day so our son could get a Catholic education. Each of the 10 families gave $10 a month for bus support and our share was Ida driving the bus. We did think about Bev and wondered what it was doing to her back but it did not hurt her as she grew almost six feet tall.

Two things happened the next year for our wheat crop. One was, since we had hay, we wanted cows and money for some better machinery. To do this we put the screws to Ida's brother Dave and demanded that he pay us the money he still had not paid when buying our home at Wardsville. Ida's dad, while in the dairy business, had Guernsey cows and Dave had purchased six heifer calves from him. He raised them to breeding age along with a white-face cow. So we bought them. He wanted to include a Guernsey bull too, but we just borrowed him instead as we didn't want a bull around any longer than needed. This got us our start in the cow-milking business one year later. And Dave was able to scrape up the money he owed us so we traded the old John Deere for a rubber-tired W-C Allis Chalmers tractor with a cultivator and a two-bottom, 14-inch Massey-Harris plow.

Brother Carl's sons were getting into the farming business in a big way and purchased a new McCormick-Deering 10-foot self-propelled combine, which would cut the wheat and thresh out the grain at the same time. So Carl had his old seven-foot Case pull-type combine for sale along with the old steel-bed manure spreader. The manure spreader was 20 years old. He asked $350 for the combine and he should have thrown in the spreader but he charged me $25 for it. He is dead now so I can say it was worn out.

Emil had the flat bed on his truck so we loaded the Allis on it and headed to Carl's farm at Williamsburg, Missouri, unloaded it and loaded the manure spreader, and Emil left for home. And me? Well I hooked the Allis (they were 15-mile-an-hour tractors on rubber) to the combine and also headed for home. The thing was about 10 feet wide. It scared the hell out of a lot of car drivers meeting me and made about the same number mad because they could not pass me as they wanted to. I have no idea of the number of miles but I would think with the shortcut through Calwood to Emil's home it surely must have been 50 miles. I would have made it all the way home earlier if not for the old narrow bridge at Jefferson City. I had to have the police escort me across because of the combine width and they made me sit there and wait from half past four o'clock until six o'clock in the evening for the traffic to thin out. I made it through Jefferson City and to Emil's before dark. This was important because the combine and tractor had no travelling or warning lights. Emil and Cath took me home and we had to unload the manure spreader anyway. The next morning Ida and I got the combine home.

So we now completed the neighborhood agreement of Bruce Cook with the corn picker, Herman Kirchhoff with the baler, and me with the combine. We could work together to get our crops taken care of but we still had the two-man operation of hay cutting.

Either in the fall of 1955 or spring of 1956 Everett and Gladys purchased the George Leonard farm and became our neighbors. They had sold the little farm of 93 acres that Everett purchased in 1936. They sold it to a dentist by the name of Dr. Reed from Jefferson City and he and his family moved into the home. Since Dr. Reed planned to enlarge the house we took the job. They extended it west and under that part made a garage. They put in subfloor over the old floor and put in rugs. They put a rock fireplace in the east room and the gable end to the north was of rock also. Clarence laid the rock and I cut the things to size with a chisel and hammer. Emil and Evy laid the brick with Emil's son Donald as mortar mixer.

At the same time, we were also building Roger and Catherine Mertens' home. Those two homes ended my home building but after that I had to work for Elmer Stockman, Jr. and Frances "Buster" Huhmann remodeling some homes in Renn's Addition. That paid for our storm windows.

Emil stayed in that line of work and Everett cut his old two-story farm house to one story, made some additions, and bricked it. It was at this home where he had his first heart attack. Gladys called me as at that time I think his children were too small to drive. On the way down to Jefferson City she wanted Emil too. Evy was coughing and after picking Emil up we took him to St. Mary's and walked him up those front steps. How he withstood that I will never know. He survived and lived for 16 more years.

Cow stanchion

We purchased 100 acres of Evy's 120 so now we owned 180 acres and we financed this portion through Moniteau Bank. We needed those acres as there was a nice creek bottom on it. We had started liming and terracing the home 80 acres and put on rock phosphate and sowed it all down in pasture and were ready for the cows as we planned on being dairymen. We were fortunate in that Mr. Cliburn also had such a plan before he sold us the farm and had taken out the horse stalls on the west side of the barn and placed in a concrete gutter and walkway. He had not poured a concrete floor between the stanchions and gutter. (A stanchion is a device that fits loosely around a cow's neck to keep the cow from moving around while it is being milked.) He had already built those the complete length of the barn. Thus we could begin milking but found that we could get a better price for Grade B milk than Grade C.

We wanted to go to Grade A but were a far way from that. Kraft Cheese in California, Missouri contacted us and told us if we put in concrete up to the stanchions they would approve us for Grade B. We did not want to use the entire length so we partitioned it for six cows. We milked by hand and used the horse trough that was by the well pump to cool the milk. Our neighbor Bruce Cook was already hauling his milk to Kraft and as he had room he hauled ours too. The only problem was carrying those buckets full of milk through the mud of winter and spring and there was a time or two when we walked right out of our boots. After all you had to save the milk.

We lucked out again because Dad quit milking and had his old International milking machine just hanging there and we thought to buy it. This was an unusual machine because the pump, motor, jars, and milkers hung on a track and you moved the entire outfit from cow to cow. Didn't have to set a bucket under the cow. To get it out of the milk barn, so he could make way for raising pigs there, he gave it to us for free as long as we removed it for him. Deal!

So far as cows go we were not too smart either as we bought the cheapest and they kicked and milked accordingly. Yet every dime we earned went into the operation and we were advancing slow and, as we thought, sure.

Spreading Cinders in Winter

IN 1958, Evy's beer-drinking buddy Rip Rannabarger, who worked as foreman for the Missouri State Highway Department maintenance shed at Centertown, wondered if a lime spreader would also spread cinders, which the highway department used in winter to provide traction on the roads in bad weather. Evy mentioned it to me and I went to see the guy, thinking of winter-time work. We both went to see the division foreman, Phil Luebbert, and he too decided it may work. The only problem was that a lime spreader fan ran at high rate of speed and spread a width of 60 feet of lime. There was no way to slow this down as it was determined by the gear ratio.

They would give us a try under the condition that we would use a cover. They would design this cover to place over the fan that slanted from both sides to the rear to knock the cinders down so they wouldn't fly out everywhere. The cover could be placed on the bed but could be removed easily after work and back to lime hauling. We took the truck to the garage on Main Street and they made the cover and installed the warning lights (amber in front and red in the rear). The red light would stay on the truck as it was used for stops along with the brake lights but the blinking yellow was to be removed when not spreading cinders and stored with the cover at the maintenance shed.

Since the old 1952 GMC had 127,000 lime-hauling miles with lots of extra motor work in spreading, I had just traded up to a 1958 GMC and needed the extra income. I had to sign a contract, if this worked out, to furnish the truck for $.12 per mile and $.65 per hour of labor. This was the going rate at that time.

The highway department used a small spreader just like the old pull-type lime spreaders we began with. They attached it to the rear of the dump beds and when raising the bed, the wheels of the spreader would touch ground providing the power to spread the cinders where needed. Then they would let the bed down to raise the spreader when it was not needed. This worked but was a darn dangerous job for the man that was riding the bed as I later found out. They did furnish dual-tire chains but these things did not last long when ice began thawing on places and we were running on bare concrete.

I ended up having a serious accident that landed me an eight-day stay in the Latham Hospital. Tony Baumgartner, who was day crew chief, had asked me to be a daytime helper. We planned to drive on Highway 50 to the U route intersection in Centertown. At that time I had never done the job before. Also at that time Highway 50 still had those curb lips on the highway edge.

Tony stopped and I climbed into the bed. He then raised the bed and I opened the chute door and when the truck hit that lip a lot of cinders shot out, choking the spreader. When that happens, you have to reach over the back of the bed and use the shovel handle to poke the cinders through. By the time I got that done the truck hit the other side lip and the same thing happened. Just when I got the thing unstopped, he dropped the bed and as I stood up he made a left turn into a driveway and I became overbalanced and fell to the pavement, landing on my head, shoulder, and side. Thank God there was a bread truck following us or else Tony, upon backing out of the driveway, would have backed right over me. That driver stopped and jumped out of his truck and then Tony realized what had happened.

They loaded me in Tony's truck and Tony took me to the hospital. I wound up with three broken ribs, a broken clavicle, and a concussion. Had a hell of a headache for several days but was soon well as ever. On going back, Tony drove by home and told Ida and she rushed right in to see me. I missed my breakfast that day. Workman's compensation paid my hospital bill and $30 per week for six weeks.

Today, after we proved these types of beds were great cinder spreaders, you see them by each highway department shed. They designed them to fit into a dump bed and use hydraulics for power and only have to hook up a hose. After a snow or ice storm they just hoist them from the bed and let them hang there until another snow. So I will say that I had a part in pioneering a great and safe idea that is a one-man operation instead of the two-man one of those years ago.

I continued working for them each winter until 1966 when I sold my truck and my nephew Jim Mertens took over with his truck. My wages went up to $.85 per hour and the truck to $.16 per mile.

The only problem was that the State paid my wages twice a month as they did the other employees. For the truck mileage payment, it had to be sent in on a purchase order and it was almost forever to get that check. In fact, I had accepted the job for winter income and we received the check when we were well into lime hauling and a shortage of money for us was no longer an issue.

Hauling Milk and Other Hard Work

EVEN WITH THE CHEAP COWS we were soon producing enough milk that Bruce Cook did not have room on his pickup, which had to be covered to meet Kraft's requirements. So we had to find another way to haul our milk.

We came up with the idea of buying a station wagon and hauling it ourselves. Besides, we needed a new car anyway as the old 1953 was, like Ida and me, getting older. We ordered a new 1961 Plymouth with built-up rear springs and larger tires and used it for hauling milk. We built a bed with steel rails so the cans would slide easily so that Ida, in a stooped position, could get them out and onto the receiving track. What a hell of a way to treat a beautiful car and it hurt, yet up came a solution. Carl had another piece of junk to sell us.

Carl was selling Grade A milk to the St. Louis market but was so far away from a milk hauler that he had to haul his milk cans to Warrenton to meet the St. Louis truck. The St. Louis market changed to bulk cooling and tanker pickup so he had his worn-out Studebaker pickup for sale. Talk about using oil; that thing just shoved in the shade the old Willys-Knight my Dad had in 1928 and the little 600 Nash I had after the war as oil users. Ida got to drive the station wagon back home from Carl's while I almost smothered to death from the oil fumes. Since Everett was a Studebaker man, we had him overhaul it to a fairly decent pickup so Ida became the pickup driver. Of course she was well experienced after driving the old school bus. She turned that bus driving job over to a neighbor lady because after all we did become well off enough to pay the $10 monthly bus dues.

Vintage Studebaker pickup

I do believe we copied Ida's dad as he was always getting into different things and as it turned out we did too. When I think about it now, it may have been that as beginning farmers you had to just to make ends meet.

So we traded the Allis, the disc, that woman-killer mower, cultivator, and plow for a Ferguson 40. We wanted a John Deere 520 instead of the Ferguson 40 but could not make a deal. One of the reasons was Ida's dad. If you did not buy a John Deere tractor or a Chevrolet car or truck you had to be crazy and it didn't bother him a bit to tell you that. So it came about that we had to disagree at times and just stood clear of him for a while.

No John Deere. So it was to Fluegel Equipment Co. who, just beginning as a Ferguson dealer, needed a sale like we needed a tractor. Along with the tractor, we wanted a three-bottom mounted plow, an eight-foot mounted disc, a seven-foot mounted field cultivator, a two-row front-mounted corn cultivator and, here Ida thanked God, also a mounted seven-foot mower. On this deal I haggled and haggled and got the trade down to $3,600 difference. I told him I would have to go to the Tipton bank to see if we could borrow the money. That night Ida and I talked this thing over and decided we could not haggle any more so I came up with the idea of a little fib. The bank said they would loan the amount of $3,600 so back to Fluegel with a lie. I could see he was eager as he said, "Ready for the deal?" and my reply was, "I'd like to, Walt, but the bank will only loan us $3,000 as they think that is what the deal difference should be." He jumped at that so we saved $600. Many people thought Walt was a little odd but that deal became a great thing for him as we later purchased over $40,000 worth of machinery from him. We always had good deals from him.

1961 Ferguson 40 tractor

This tractor had lights so I would haul lime during the day and get wheat land ready to sow at night. By renting land Ida and I put out 90 acres of wheat. I had gotten all the land plowed. I put the disc on the tractor for her and she would disc all that day. I would dismount the disc after supper and that night we would sow wheat, she riding the drill to note if it was sowing and me driving and filling the drill with seed and fertilizer. Of course this nighttime work was after the family, kids and all, did the milking.

With all that wheat to combine along with that of Bruce Cook and Herman Kirchhoff, we decided to overhaul the motor on the old pull-type combine and had a friend do that work. When he was almost finished he needed some new parts and on a day of rain I headed to

Jefferson City to the Case dealer, Raithel Brothers, and ran into some old time friends, one of whom, Corny, married my distant kinfolk Leo Scheuler's daughter.

Well I got those parts and while visiting I noted an almost new Case S.P. 9 self-propelled combine that had been traded in on a new 10-foot cut with a two-row corn picker-sheller by a fellow named Gentres who was a bottom farmer and needed the corn head. The S.P. 9 was built before this idea and could not be equipped so. I called the man and he told me it was just like new and would be a good buy if one did not want a picker. Again Ida and I got our heads together and decided to buy it because of slack lime hauling and it could be a great money maker (never mind how much additional work it would be for us). That type of combining was a great thing beginning then and since most farmers hauled their grain with their pickups, I would take my truck along and put wheat on it while they were taking the pickup loads to market. Every evening I would have a load of wheat on my truck to haul and that much more money to make. Believe me, that combine took me north to Jamestown and as far east as the Jefferson City Country Club. In the fall it combined Lespedeza, clover, and milo.

Getting New Cows

THE OLD MILKING MACHINE had the jars hanging from the carrier so we could put a scale there and decided to treat our poor cows better than ourselves by feeding them according to the amount of milk they gave. Ida and I also decided to get some better cows, specifically the Brown Swiss breed as Ida's uncle Al Markway and the Henry LePage family were doing good with them, both in milking and marketing breeding animals. So we began with four of them. We especially liked the fact that they were calm and their production was much better than those we were milking. We learned later that this was the wrong choice for us.

Brown Swiss cow [6]

I need to back up and get this in the story. When we formed the McGirk Bus Company I was elected treasurer and the decision was to do the banking business with the Moniteau National Bank. Since Ida did the collecting and the depositing and I the check writing, both of us made friends with the nicest and best banker ever. His name was Robert "Bobby" Hurt. We learned that he was willing to go to bat for us with the directors when buying the land from Everett. He was cashier so we changed our banking business from Tipton so as not to have to make separate trips.

Beverly, age three, feeding a calf

In the meantime, our kids were working their butts off right along with Ida and me. We thought we should do something for them and the two of us came up with the idea to help them get in the cow business when they started high school. When David decided to go to high school, we told him that he was to buy a cow and go to the bank to finance it. So the 14-year-old boy discussed this with his vocational agricultural teacher from Future Farmers of America (FFA), Mr. Denker, who advised David to buy a good Holstein, which would not be a cheap cow. We told him he had to borrow the money and if the banker agreed I would talk with him. So the scared kid went to Mr. Hurt at the bank and told him he wanted to purchase a good cow and was asked how much a good cow would cost. Mr. Hurt agreed it was to be a good one.

I then went in to talk with Mr. Hurt and told him that we would see that David would pay off the note as promised. We told him that we had made an agreement with all four of our children that we would feed and take care of two cows for them for their help to us and that they would have to use half of the milk check to pay for the cow and the other half for their clothing and school expense. When they got the first cow paid for, they then could have the second.

David then made his first purchase of a registered cow, Van Fel Magic Queen, from Vanderfeltz dairy farm and he paid what Ida and I thought was a fantastic price. It was $450, but that cow proved to the entire family that all of our cows were to be Holsteins and got us into being Registered Holstein breeders. Although David's cow had all bull calves, he traded the first one back to the Vanderfeltz dairy farm for a heifer calf which was to become his second cow. Believe this, this calf became sick and died on the day President Kennedy was assassinated after all our work trying to save it.

Holstein cow [7]

We then decided not to depend on calves for the second cow and purchased another like the first one. We followed this practice through with all four children. The two cows furnished all the money we could afford for their education and amounted to, at that time, from $1,200 to $1,500 per year. The kids also understood that if they wanted a college education there would be no car or stereo until they were juniors in college. Any other college expense was to come from work and scholarships.

One of our registered heifers

We sold our herd before Bev finished college so we estimated the amount the other children received and paid that amount to her. All realized that when they became 21 this would stop and at that time the ownership of the cows would revert back to us. Although at that time we did not think about it, the beauty of this was that paying for the cows gave them a good credit rating with the bank. When the time came for a car, they could finance it with Mr. Hurt and this was of great help to them.

Sometimes I think Mr. Hurt thought he was more a father to our kids than I was.

Making Improvements

WE BEGAN SOME WORK that made our home decent to live in. We had Emil cover our home with asbestos siding and thereby avoided painting, and with tar paper it also became insulation. A neighbor, Mr. Fred Maier, who was a painter, painted the exposed wood white and the roof with aluminum paint. This home was built in 1912 and I was told by the Kirchhoff family who built it that the roof was put on the home by Frankie Schmidt's dad from St. Thomas. This was the roof that he invented and obtained a patent for. It was nailed along the board on the sheeting edges and went the entire width of the building and never had nail showing on the roof. It was crimped over the other edge and nailed there. Although we had the roof painted twice in our 24 years (second time with metallic zinc oxide as the aluminum didn't last) that roof is still on the home after 81 years. Compare that to roofs of today.

We had Scheidt's Hardware and Gas put in two gas furnaces and a 500-gallon propane tank. They had put in a metal flue as the old brick unlined flues were bad. A couple of years later the insurance company inspected the home for insurance renewal and told us we would have to replace the flues. I told them that we already had with the metal one. They said, "We know that, but since those old flues are there you may decide to put in a wood stove." I suppose they thought I was even crazier than I always thought I was. We did not want to tear out the flues because of the wallpaper and mess, so they compromised. I had to take them down below roof level and put new tin over the holes. Well, I know I am not smart, but that beat all.

Now came another job for Emil and that was to extend our corn crib and granary long enough for a shed for my truck. There was a hallway between the granary and corn crib, wide enough for a wagon, that we used for the car although it was so narrow that you could not get in or out of it. So we tore the crib out since we no longer gathered ear corn. Just kept right on going long enough to cover the self-propelled combine too. I mentioned the insurance man thinking we were crazy. I will now prove his point. The darn truck was longer than the granary width so we had to put a lean-to along the south side. More expense but at least now we had a place for the tractor too. To make matters worse, the combine was too tall so we ended up digging a trench for each wheel. Oh well! For the pickup, Clarence Veit built a new dairy milking parlor with a garage. We tried our best, yet there was always something sitting out in the weather.

Done a little thinking here too. An elevated four-cow in-line bypass, so we could turn each cow out after she finished milking and enter another and get her ready to be milked. This saved time. The elevation was four blocks high, putting the cow's udder at arm height, so we would not have to stoop while milking.

Cows walking up steps

The building was 24 feet wide with a four-inch concrete dividing wall between the garage, milk room, and feed room. The length was 40 feet with a 10 by 20 foot holding area on the east end that was sheltered by a lean-to cover. The dividing wall was offset from the center so as to give us 12 feet of clearance. Along the south wall we placed four stalls beginning two feet from the east wall with steps so we could get to the walkway that was used by the cows to enter each stall. This was done because sometimes a cow would refuse to enter a stall (especially a new one) so in that case you could boot them in the butt. You could also block the cow off to artificially inseminate her. The remaining length was used as steps down with a south door to exit. Yes, a cow can walk up and down steps just like a person can.

Another four-block-high row of eight-inch concrete blocks beginning two feet from the east end and six feet from the south wall was the elevated portion of the milking parlor. In the south wall an equal height four-inch-wide block was set in instead of an eight-inch one and this provided a "notch" for the stall floor to rest on for extra support. This area accounted for a lot of rock hauling to fill it and a lot of work for me.

Elevated milking parlor

Clarence Veit built it for us, along with his workers Dave Braun and a Lueckenotte son. Walters Masonry Company of Centertown who also did the brickwork on their homes laid the concrete blocks.

When we got that area full, Clarence poured the concrete, putting beer bottles where the milking stall posts would be placed to serve as circular forms. He got them just where they were supposed to be too. Did you ever have to break a beer bottle out of concrete that you had to put a steel post into? Try it sometime but, when using that chisel, watch your eyes because of that flying glass.

Since Dave took welding at Vo-Ag, we made those stanchions out of used well pipe. Where did we get that pipe from? Most of it came out of the well when we put the plastic hose in, or I should say put two plastic hoses in. That came about because there were no submersible pumps in our day. Now a two-stage jet used a one-inch plastic pipe to force water down to a jet installed in the bottom of the well and the water passing through that jet sent an inch and a half diameter stream of water back. Don't ask me how it worked because I cannot tell you. I can tell you that it took a smart man to get it primed and pressure built up and that smart man had to be me. Darn. After starting it by letting a dribble into the tank for pressure, then after about five tries you got it going. That is, if you held down that dribble enough to begin with. Well! The thing was still working when we sold the farm some 16 years later.

Do you think you had it hard in life? Try digging up and pulling a 120-foot length of double hose out of a well to put in a splicer every time that first plastic pipe split and lost pressure, and you ask me how I learned to cuss.

One thing, this cussing experience learned me how to get some new decent well pipe from Scruggs-Guhlman Lumber Company for free because I used some of my colorful new language. He was probably shaking like a leaf on a tree during a wind storm when I got through. You know what? He gave me the best pipe ever because it lasted for over 15 years. It was still in use after we left the farm. In the dairy business it pumped a hell of a lot of water, and that included the home. We did take a bath once in a while (if we had time) and the stool was well used too, especially at night. If you were out working on the farm you just "went" where you were and that saved on fertilizer.

Next, we dug a trench silo out behind the chicken house and had a neighbor by the name of Clarence Sappington chop the corn for silage. The chopped corn went into the trench silo and was packed down to get rid of any air pockets to start the fermentation process in which it became silage. The nutrients in the corn were preserved in the silage so it could be fed to the cows in the winter when the pasture wasn't as good. Got more milk out of the cows that way.

After all those improvements, we thought the farm was in pretty good shape.

Buying Farm Equipment

THE SONS OF OUR NEIGHBOR, Herman Kirchhoff with the John Deere cross-mount hay baler, decided there were easier ways to make a living than farming so they took jobs away from home. Herman was having trouble with his baler and thought he was not mechanical enough to run it but really the trouble was because his sons had torn it all to hell. Of course he helped with that too.

We were baling alfalfa hay in the bottom land we got from Evy when the roller chain that times the needles used to insert the wires came apart. Thus the baler became out of time. Herman went home and got the book to re-time it. The book said, and it emphasized in heavy black letters, that the plunger had to be on the compression stroke when the needles were entering the bale chamber. Herman said anybody with any sense knows that the needle could not enter when the plunger was on compression and promptly had the needles coming in as the plunger was coming back.

The darn thing baled two bales and when the bale filled the chamber and began to get pressure it slipped the big V belt. Instead of stopping to see what was wrong he just sat on the tractor and rammed and rammed the needles until they looked like a snake. He went to John Deere at Tipton for new ones and found they cost $38 each. Of course he thought that was too much so we tried to straighten them with a hammer and post maul and he expected that to work.

John Deere had a unique tying system as what was called a needle was a pressed steel oval with a flare on top and in this flare were two small rollers. Now the why of the needles coming in the bale chamber was this. As the plunger compressed the hay, the needles came up through a slot in the plunger and pushed the two wires in a shaft that had a U and that shaft spun around about 20 times twisting the wire and then putting a kink while breaking it to keep it from unwinding. Since the two needles with their two rollers each took a lot of pressure, there was a lift arm on each side of the bale chamber. The geared shaft had three quarter-inch soft bolts as a safety shear and these had been replaced with steel bolts. When ramming the needles, instead of shearing, those steel bolts twisted the shaft.

It was Herman's decision to use only the side without the twist. Even with this the poor thing did bale hay. He turned the thing over to me to run but then for some reason the bale length control quit working. While I was mostly looking to follow the windrow (the narrow row of hay formed by the side rake) I looked back and I had a bale about 50 feet long. It came out the side of the baler and made a curve and just followed along. The sad thing about the whole affair was that the baler looked like a new one and had probably baled 10,000 bales without missing a one. What a shame and by this time I was angry.

Since we were baling high-quality alfalfa it was ruining fast so I called another distant neighbor by the name of Vernon Messerli, who had a T-24 twine-tying John Deere, to finish our crop and also for the balance of the season. Somehow Herman Kirchhoff's son Ted got the thing working. There was no way we would take a chance on it.

We also traded the Case combine for a new John Deere self-propelled combine because I wanted a corn-picker head. While Clarence was building the milk house, I shelled the corn crop that David had put out on land he rented from Ebenezer Porter.

When the milking barn was completed, David and I (as I mentioned before) built the stanchions and put up the track for the old milker and now we could at least stand up while milking. I saw a nice used Chevrolet pickup in Jefferson City, so I traded the Studebaker and when David turned 16 he and Ted became the milk haulers, relieving Ida of that job. We were coming up in the world. Oh my!

This too! In 1962 we traded the old 1958 GMC for a two and a half ton GMC, put a 12-inch riser on the bed, and could now scale eight tons of lime. Did I learn a lesson here! All the other truckers became jealous and demanded we all haul the same size loads to be fair. The men who did not want the expense of a higher-priced truck demanded that I could earn no more than they. Never mind that I was willing to risk the added expense to advance myself. Now our President says that we who did are "greedy" and should share what we worked our butts off for with those who just sat on their butts. To make this fair, his idea is to use taxes to even us up.

The year 1964 saw a new 65 Massey-Ferguson replace the smaller 40. A 30 as a smaller one for lighter duty and cleaning the barn lot was added.

Emil decided to quit farming so he offered David his John Deere machinery. He made him a real good deal of the 620 tractor, wheel-mounted disc, cultivator, three-bottom plow and the best of all: a mounted manure loader. Just think of all the pitchforks we set aside. Yet this loader later became a problem when we got concrete. David thought he might become a farmer and jumped at the chance as the complete outfit could be purchased on a note at the unbelievable low price of $4,200. Thank you Emil and Cath.

Came the year 1965 and since we now had three tractors and two large enough we purchased a silage chopper and along with our own chopping did custom work for others too. Combine and chopper were two more ways to become more "greedy."

Now here comes Herman Kirchhoff wanting to sell me that old baler. Made me a good deal there too. He would sell the baler and side-delivery rake for $550 and we wouldn't even have to have money. Just "bale" it out by doing his baling. Who in the hell would want that outfit? So we put all our heads together and told him this. We would buy the outfit if we could trade it off and still do his deal. He said he did not give a damn so long as we did his baling.

He did not know I had approached Fluegel and was offered more than $1,000 on a trade for a new McCormick-Deering No. 56 (commercial baler, large bales). It had killed a man and Fluegel had traded a Massey-Ferguson for it as the owner no longer wanted it on his farm. It had been owned by a man named Kempker at Henley. It had its own motor and his hired hand thought he heard an unusual noise that sounded like it was coming from underneath the baler. He stopped the tractor and throttled down the motor. Promptly got down and stuck his head under the crank bearing of the plunger shaft and since it ran near the ground it crushed his head. When Kempker found him, the baler was running slow and just continued to beat his head to a pulp. Because it had killed a man did not bother me. I thought if I were dumb enough to put my head underneath as he did that I was hard-headed enough that instead of crushing my head the baler would just jump up and down. It would think it was beating on a rock.

Hauling lime, hauling cinders, milking cows, chopping silage, combining, and now hay baling—we needed something else to do. Oh yeah! We had lots of it. Now don't begin to roll up your pants leg thinking you are standing in it. Really! What I have been telling you is the truth. We really did all the things I'm telling you and even more. I am not handing you a line of manure.

Now comes old Herman Kirchhoff again and this time he wants to sell us 80 acres of land that adjoined us to the east. It was an original part of our farm. He was riding with me when I was combining his oats and he gave us a decent price. It rained while we were eating dinner so I had to quit and go home. Again we talked this over and decided to buy it. Went to the banker and he said okay. Thinking we would settle the deal when it became dry enough to combine again I waited until then. Well Bruce Cook got wind of this and went to see Herman and said he was here the longest and offered him more money. When I told Herman we would buy he answered, "I guess I made you mad at me but I sold it to Bruce." My answer was that it was not my land and was his to do with as he wanted to. He told me then that we would have first offer when he sold the home place. I told him okay, but to sell it to someone else if he expected me to pay additional for the house as it would be of no use to us. I didn't give a darn.

The 65 Ferguson went so we could get an even larger tractor yet. We stepped up to an 85 Massey-Ferguson. Wow! This one even had two exhaust stacks right up there in the air and I thought I was a kid again. I never had anything to hotrod with and now I could dream as that old boy was "talking" to me. Reminded me of the days setting on Carl's W-40 and as that was a six it really purred. No wonder I'm deaf.

Becoming Big Shots

SINCE WE WERE ON OUR WAY to becoming big shots, we decided to go all out on cow milking. That meant another can cooler along with the one we already had. A DeLaval cow-to-can pipeline milker with an in-line strainer. This thing sat on six 10-gallon cans and as it filled one it just went on to the next. That only cost us $4,200.

Pass-through from garage to cooler

Now what was really nice was something I thought up all by myself and this made Dave and Ted so happy. When building, I'd had Clarence put a door between the garage and milk room. Thereby you could carry the milk cans to the pickup. My idea was to knock out those concrete blocks above that door and put a two by four header there. That was equal to the two-inch track. I then made the door long enough to meet under the header and still had the milk room pass inspection. Got a new ball bearing wire stretcher and made a thing like they used to carry block ice with. Then the boys could just pick up a can out of the cooler and roll it through the door and set it on the pickup.

When milking, after the cans were full, it was used to put the cans in the cooler. It even made the girls happy as it made them "man enough" to do men's work too.

We were all so pleased about this easy way of doing work that we were willing to add 10 more cows and all that extra work to pay for the thing. As our new President says, "That is technology at work." Hell, we were 30 years ahead of him.

Next I was elected to the County Extension Board and thereby got in with the big boys of the University of Missouri College of Agriculture, School of Agricultural Economics and signed an agreement with them. They had just procured a computer so big it took a whole room for itself. It got real hot and I believe it used tubes as it was before transistors or microchips. It was probably just as slow as I was and not even much smarter.

I had to sign a contract that I would furnish them all my farm and home records, expenses, and income. Everything was reported to them by code numbers furnished to me. We had to let them use those records to teach students Agricultural Economics and there were 10 farms paired for comparison. Believe me when I tell you, this was the smartest move that Bud Mertens ever made. We began to learn what farming was all about.

Everything we did at work for each item—baling, crops, milk, sale of animals, fence building, tractor work, etc., labor too, interest, and money borrowed—was examined. This told us that milk cows were the way to go as they outperformed all the custom work that we were killing ourselves doing. It didn't take us long to write a letter to our customers telling them to find someone else. We could keep that machinery setting on our farm for our own use and put all that effort in cows. We sold the truck and this was in 1966.

We then put the work into cows, building them up to a high producing herd, and reached the point where some of our registered cows were in the top 2% of the Holstein breed.

We had already installed automatic feeders in the milking parlor. All we had to do was set a dial to feed according to milk production. To be as accurate as possible we joined the University of Missouri Dairy Herd Improvement Association and thereafter the herd was serviced by a technician who weighed the milk and tested the butter fat content. This took away the possibility that someone could cheat (not us!). It also qualified us for the requirements of the Registered Holstein Association and thereafter all milk production was entered on the cow's record. Also the calving interval, and this was used to promote the registered bulls' records. This information showed if a bull improved milk and butter fat production, and if not you could avoid his use. However, some of the bulls with low production could be high in cow conformity for classification. An example: If you had a cow with excellent production but an udder that could not handle it, it would then be better to knock her production so her offspring could have udder quality. One of the things we can brag on was we had high classification on udder quality and a cow is only as good as her udder. Through those years we brought our herd average from just over 9,000 pounds per cow to almost 17,000 on our registered cows. While we were doing this we also upped the cow quality. We learned the value of this when we had our dispersal sale in 1974 when we got out of dairy farming.

David and I also trained for artificial insemination so we could use frozen semen from high-production and high-conformity bulls. We kept a pickup bull for heifers.

Herman sold his farm to two of his sons. One was progressive and the other was like Herman. They could not get along so the progressive one turned his half over to the other and since he could not make a living at it he sold it to us. We gave him $8,000 for the 120 acres and now we owned 300 acres. Put a bulldozer in there for a couple of months and cleaned out a hell of a lot of fences to make the fields into large ones from the many pens he had. This also included terracing and liming, phosphating and fertilizing to soil test. We needed the extra pasture too.

Aerial view of farm with boundaries marked

1954
Purchased 80 acre farm including
AR John Deere Tractor and rigid beam
Oliver plow - Floyd Cilburn - $5500.00

1960
Purchased 100 acres including barn
from E. A. Mertens - $6000.00

1962
Purchased 120 acres including all
buildings from Ted Kirchoff $8000.00

1968
Purchased 40 acres including all
buildings from Fred Maier $4200.00

TOTAL $23,700.00
SOLD 100 ACRES 1974 - BAL. 1978

List of acreage purchases

David and I made a feeding manger along the county road. We made a new-style rack through which the cows placed their heads to get at the hay. Cows had a bad habit of pulling hay through a rack and wasting it by treading on it and then going after more. It was learned that if the rack was on a slant the cow would have to turn her head to get to the hay. When they tried to back away they would bump their head and learned to keep it by the feed in the first place. It was installed in concrete and every 10 feet we placed a post and this too was welded on the slant. We made these long enough to hold up a shed to cover the manger.

Our new manger

The family poured 12 feet of concrete for the cows to stand on while eating. This concrete slab caused a problem when we loaded manure as it was juicy and the John Deere loader with the mechanical bucket which was set with a suction to dig caused all the manure to run off it before you got to the manure spreader. We made a trip to the John Deere dealer at Jamestown and traded the old 620 and the loader for a new 2020 with a quick-detach loader and this bucket was built such that it could be tilted to dig, carry, and unload by a hydraulic cylinder. The old one had a narrow bucket and this was also a problem because the tractor wheels were wider than the bucket. The new one was ordered with a one-yard bucket and was equal to the width of the wheels.

We also purchased outright a new Plymouth four-door with a 383-cubic-inch motor, power for an automatic transmission and, of all things, an air conditioner. Kept the old station wagon for a car for our son Ted. It was six years old and only had 77,000 miles on it. Our new car—well, Karen had to use it for a school function. I told her it had enough gas for the trip. I think she wanted to do a little cruising. While backing to the electric gas pump (we had one of those too) and looking back to not hit the pump she promptly hit a tree with the left front fender. A brand new car already bent up. Oh well! Life goes on.

Cows, Cows, and More Cows

Driving Cattle

NOW WE HAD THREE FARMS, three pastures, and three sets of cows. Every time a calf was born, if it was not a bull, we took a photograph of it and put the date of birth on the photo. This was necessary to obtain registry because in that way the animal could be identified. We also did this with the grade animals, with only one purebred parent. The calves were kept on the home place until they were three months old. We had a chute by the calf pen and used the trailer Ted built and that worked keen. Once a month we had our family get-together and this was not to party, although a great dinner was furnished. The kids in college and the kids not in college and Mom and Pop went to work in this way.

Our calves

We had purchased another 40-acre farm that joined the land we purchased from Evy. We did this to keep a man who was a hog farmer from getting it. He was not a fence builder and we knew there would be a problem. We joined these two farms together and had the greatest amount of pasture there so the largest animals were put there along with a bull. Since there was a bull with these heifers I think you know what took place and that was intended to get a cow in milk production. (Did the bull have a little fun? I dunno, but I do know he got pretty possessive and angry when you took some of his harem away.)

That bull had our prefix and his name was Mertens Supreme Mr. Joe. The Mertens name got spread all over the country when we had our cattle sale. But this bull got mean. After several close calls and with him getting me down one time we decided to take him to market. He weighed over 2,400 pounds and was sold as a bologna bull. After all sale expenses, he cleared us the amount of $942. I am not pulling your leg by handing you a line of bull. Just a lot of bologna and not baloney. Got that? Okay! Now I can proceed.

We once had a bull jump over the stock rack of our truck. This bull was a noted fence jumper. It was on a day that our milk tester was with us overnight. I had gone into the house to clean up to take the bull to Columbia. As the tester was leaving, he shouted, "The bull is jumping out of the truck!" He was having trouble getting it done, but his hind hoofs caught that two-by-four placed in trucks for double decking and he was able to push himself over. Thank God it was at home. Ida and I placed two gates on top of the truck and wired them down. Reloaded him to be a hamburger bull and got just over $700 for him. I suppose they did not want "tough" hamburger.

The first thing we did during our monthly family get-together was go to the large heifer farm (those with the bull) and those that were "springing" (near calving) were removed to home and fed to get them ready for calving and milk production. Of course they had to be separated from the others and driven down the road to home. This took every member of the family (and there was a time or two when we even wished we had more kids). Unless you take the whole herd, cows simply do not want to go where you want them to.

Then we proceeded to the Kirchhoff farm. Using the pictures and birth dates we separated all those 16 months of age and drove them to the breeding heifer farm from which we had removed the first group. These two moves were the hardest darn day of work ever and we were dumb enough to call it our day of family outing. Well, my knee hurt like hell and I suppose I was the one sitting around pouting. What was so odd, that knee quit hurting for years and to make up for that now hurts to the point of using that kid word of "ouch" out loud and under your breath "damn." No, I did not use God before it.

Moving Up to Grade A Milk

I NEED TO GO BACK NOW to our relations with Kraft Foods. They had one of the smartest and best men working for them as a field man—Dan McGrath. Both he and the company had their heart in our interest. We have many photos of him and our awards from Kraft. Every so often there is such a man (include me, please).

Ida and me reviewing farm records with Dan McGrath, 1965

Dan was there for the move from the Grade B hand-milking to the new milk parlor. For the milk coolers as against the old stock tank. The cow-to-can milker. And then the time he worked us toward and to a bulk tank. He traded in the old can coolers, cans, and the cow-to-can deal on a 300-gallon bulk milk tank. This bulk milk went directly to the Kraft Cheese Plant at Eldon. No more pickup truck milk hauling for the sons as both were in college. Ida says thank you Dan, because without that change she would have had to go back to milk hauling. Maybe Karen and Bev could have done it but we did not want to ask them to add this chore. Both were taking care of calves before and after school.

Shortly after our changeover, Dan died of a heart attack while standing on the porch of a dairyman by the name of Stahl. Dan was only 43 years old and a skinny guy and no one would have expected his death in this way.

Five short months after installing the bulk milk handling, we went to Grade A milk to Jefferson City for the extra income. If Dan had not died, we would not have thought to make that change. We thought that much of him—it would almost have felt a betrayal. But alas, after his death we had to move on and so we moved on to selling milk to Jefferson City.

Remodeling Our House

IDA GOT TIRED OF OUR CLOSET-TYPE KITCHEN CABINETS so we finally got around to replacing them. Her brother Leroy wanted Saturday work and so we hired him, and sometimes a young son came along to help or play. At the same time we took out the old from-kitchen-to-bathroom window that had been painted white.

Leroy built a new set of kitchen cabinets that were built right. He even left a space that was a perfect fit for a stove. The old Magic Chef stove then went to the storm cellar to can on. Now we had a pump, a hot water heater, washing machine with two wash tubs, the stove, a potato box that was up from the floor on one end, and shelves on both sides for the canned food, of which there was much of, in that cellar. That outdoor cellar was so crowded that though Ida could still turn around in it, me, since I got fat, why I had to walk in and had to back out. Not enough room there for me to turn.

Under the potato bin was enough room for eight gallons of grape wine that someone told Ida how to make. The trouble was no one would try drinking it. We had grapevines, a pear tree (until a windstorm blew it down), a cherry tree and the birds got most of them, and last, lots of blackberries along with gooseberries too. Good gosh. Forgot the three peach trees and will add the biggest garden in the area. A 'tater patch too.

Now that wine was made some way in gallon jugs and was capped. I thought it may explode but it never did. It started out purple and eight years later was just as clear as could be. One Sunday Dad and Mom came for a visit and Ida asked Dad if he would like to try it. To him it was so good that he took all eight gallons back with him. Well I'll say this about Dad and the wine: Life may not begin at 40 for those who went like 60 when they were 20. That wine made him think he was young again. Poor Mom. Just think about Dad thinking he was young again. Weeooo.

Our cabinets looked so good that we had to do the floor. Put on a new subfloor and those square tiles. As we were doing the floor, we added a new electric clothes dryer. Had to get that before we got all the tile laid as you know the things do need electricity and a four-inch pipe to let the steam out, and both had to go under the floor. At least now the kitchen was pretty and the bathroom too without the old window.

Ida helped me by day and in return I had to help her at night. Now don't get smart ideas. What I mean is help her fix up the house nice at night.

The house had lots of doors; in fact, too many doors for Ida. A front door and two back doors to the porches. Now those two doors left from the kitchen. Maybe the previous owners thought they could not get out of the house fast enough in case of a fight. To help in this regard they put a door from the parlor (people who think their ship came in usually find it to be a hardship and that was us) to the one porch and for the other porch a door from the living room.

One porch was already the bathroom and the other was enclosed with storm windows and after borrowing $360 from my veteran's insurance became our deep freezer room. For boots too. Since two doors to the bathroom are risky (someone may slip in on you), this door was removed and covered by a sheet of plywood on the bathroom side. This left the whole door jamb open on the living room side and old Clem had to make a magazine rack on the bottom and above that a series of whatnot shelves. This looked so good that the door from the parlor to the freezer room was removed just like the other but the bottom here had a newspaper rack plus those shelves. All of this was because we were self-made but only the rich will admit it. Am I showing off?

When we bought the place, we pulled thousands of nails from the floors when we first moved in because of the nailed-down rugs and linoleum. Worked our butts off sanding those old floors and after varnishing them admired their beauty, nail holes and all, and now darn if we didn't cover all that beauty with a subfloor and rugs. Good gosh and all!

That didn't satisfy Ida though, as there was more. Our front door came into a four by six-foot space and to the right was a door into the parlor and to the left was a door into the living room. (When we got richer this room was then called the TV room as we could afford a TV.) We removed these two doors as well. Straight ahead was the stairway to the upper and only bedrooms. At the top of the stairs straight ahead was a door to our bedroom. To the right was a hallway the entire length to a door on the west end and this was the boys' room. Just above the stairway was another four-foot square landing and from this a door led into the girls' room. For all the rooms there was only one puny closet and that one closet was why it was our room.

Well everybody knows that there had to be more closets. So in the boys' room along the entire wall we put a closet, a real big one, and this big closet had to have its two doors. Now the girls' room also had to have a big closet and it had two doors too. These big closets had to handle their clothes with enough room left for storing the summer clothing during the winter and the winter clothing during the summer. The four doors we'd removed downstairs were used for the closet doors upstairs.

Since all visitors would come in the front door, that little space the width of the stairway was covered with linoleum and that was called the "mud room." Of course from the mud room there stood that stairway that all could see so it had to have carpeting too. At that time the sidewalk led to the road and any parking area was by the milk house so everybody coming for a visit came into the house through the kitchen door. This after we had fixed up the front entrance so pretty. Be assured the sidewalk made a change too but that was later.

The Fall

WHEN YOU ARE FLYING HIGH there comes a fall that brings a halt to those high-flying dreams you had. Darn it to hell anyway.

In late October of 1967 at about three o'clock I went to the barn (the one on Evy's place) to get the next morning's hay. I was using the little tractor and the FFA trailer Ted had built as it held 20 bales of hay, the amount that we fed. I had opened the door and backed the tractor and trailer right up against it to make the hay loading easy.

I then climbed up to the top of the barn, threw the 20 bales down, and proceeded to the barn ladder. This ladder was made of one by four boards that were nailed to a 10-inch post that supported the roof. Also there was a 10 by 10 square beam that tied the barn together, about 14 feet above the hallway. This barn did not have a loft and was so old that it was of the time when you drove a wagon through and threw the loose hay from the wagon. Thus the hallway. It was built like the barn my brother Emil burned on the Luebbering farm all those years ago when he was four years old.

As I was coming down the ladder and came to that crossbeam I worked myself around it. I must have stepped on the outer end of one of those boards and I suppose because of age it had dry rot. Either way, it broke and I slid all the way down, landing on my feet and it felt just as if someone poured hot water down my spine. Of course my legs collapsed and when I landed on my butt I had that same feeling again. Two things saved me. One was that the board that broke was not at the top and the second was that there was lots of loose hay to land on. Thank God those hay bales I had thrown down were not there either.

To be honest, my fall could not have been over 10 feet.

I really got sick to my stomach and just lay there, thinking someone would come for me. Then I had another thought, and that was if they did, it would be sometime later. I tried to get on my feet and found that I could not. I then crawled to the doorway and used that to get on my feet but there stood that darn trailer. I thought I would die before I got over the rack and back to the ground although I had done that many times after loading it with hay.

I made it to the tractor and got on it and headed for home. Since we had heifers in the pasture there, I thought I should shut the gate but found I could not. That little old tractor had an iron seat and it bounced me so bad that I could not stand the pain. I stood up and drove. (The county had just graded the road and pushed a gravel windrow along the right side). To make matters worse, here came the school bus and I got as near as I could to that windrow but the SOB driver just kept honking his horn and made me jump that windrow too. After dropping off the kids he came back and it was the same thing all over again. (I drove a truck enough that I know he could have made it by.) I feel that he was using his authority as a school bus driver and that he thought he was something special.

I made it home and off the tractor and to the steps. But since we had no guardrail to grasp I could not make it up those three steps. I called out for Ida and she came to help me into the house. We thought I had only a bad back sprain. I lay on the couch and Ida and the girls went out to get the hay and close the gate. They also did the milking. When the chores were done we had supper and I lay down again. At about nine o'clock Ida said, "It's bedtime," and believe this, she had to help me up those steps and to bed. It was not the best night, yet I did sleep.

The next morning they again did the milking and the girls went to school. After Ida got the equipment washed and the barn cleaned, she loaded me up and drove the nine miles to town and the doctor. When we told him what had happened, he said, "I will not even take an X-ray," and just called an ambulance and sent me to Dr. Shull at Memorial Hospital in Jefferson City. The Bowlin Brothers took me down, charging $5, and rolled that gurney into emergency and, again believe this, made me walk to the X-ray room. Jack Bowlin said to them, "That man may have a broken back," but that made no difference. It did though, after the X-rays showed that my back was broken in two places and that I had suffered a compression on the 10th vertebra. The vertebra that joined my pelvic saddle was crushed; it skipped the next one and the next was split. I'm telling you I had 18 miserable days in the hospital.

This made it pretty tough for the Mertens family. Karen and Bev were still in high school and, as Karen had taken drivers training, they stayed to help Ida do the milking and then headed for school. They used the new Plymouth as it was automatic and Karen could drive it to school but many times they were tardy. That left Ida with the old stick-shift station wagon to use on her visits to me. Although I asked her not to, she came every day to see me.

I mentioned earlier that when I told Rose that Ida and I were getting married she told me I didn't know how lucky I was to get that girl. This one period truly proved those words as I do not think any other person could have done what she did. She got all the milk work done: she cleaned the equipment, milked 65 cows, and cleaned the milk barn. She then took the Kelly-Ryan self-unloading silage wagon to the trench silo, forked two tons of silage on it, and then fed part of it to the two groups of heifers, bringing the rest home for the dairy cows. Then she had to clean up for the visit with me. By the time she got back home it was milking time again. My two sons came home from college every other day to get the hay home.

As for me, I was strapped to a curved board. Dr. Shull said he did not want to put me in a body cast; he preferred a body brace instead. He had me measured to have one made and that would take three days.

Dr. Shull told me that with a spinal injury I would lose the ability to urinate or have bowel action at about the same time. So he made arrangements for an orderly to insert a catheter but the orderly could not get it into my bladder. In my fall, when landing on my butt, I must have injured my prostate because it had swelled to the point of completely closing my urinary canal. They called Dr. Shull back and he and the orderly placed what he called a hook (to me this looked like a curved steel bar) inside of the catheter and just forced this thing into my bladder. I suppose the idea was that the hook would come back, leaving the catheter in place. This did not happen as the catheter tube came right back with it. By that time I really wanted to die. Then it was decided to ream my prostate. Dr. Shull gave me a shot in the arm so I was half asleep but I felt every bit of it. This whole thing started at half past 10 o'clock in the morning and lasted until two o'clock in the afternoon. After all of this they did get my bladder relief, but since this was done in my room I got the worst urinary tract infection a person could ever get.

I also had an angry roommate because he missed his dinner and a visit from his wife and believe me he let Dr. Shull know it all the time he was working with me. The doctor ignored him and afterwards hung a "no visitor" sign on the door. Of course this stopped a visit for me also as Willard and Gerri were there to see me, as was Ida.

My roommate was a fellow who worked for Gwen Braun's husband on the Missouri State Highway Department bridge crew. He had been guiding a steel beam that was being placed and the crane operator dropped it the last 10 inches and before he could turn it loose it snapped the vertebra just above his pelvic saddle too. This happened sometime before my accident, as he already had this vertebra fused by taking a piece of his pelvic bone. While I was with him they placed him in a cast that encased his body and extended down his right leg to his knee. He was then ready to be released to go home. His wife came after him while Dr. Shull was with me and I remember what Dr. Shull said. This was a young couple and as he was hopping around on his "stiff" leg and showing his wife how good he could get around, she said (in front of both Dr. Shull and me), "Honey, how on earth are we going to make love with that thing on?" Dr. Leslie was his doctor.

When they left the room Dr. Shull said to me, "In about three days when he begins itching under that cast the last thing he will think about is making love. That itching will drive him crazy and that's why I didn't encase you in one." I hardly felt like laughing because I was blew up with so much gas yet I did have a good belly shaker. I suppose that good laugh helped me along.

On Monday morning the man from St. Louis brought my body brace in and put it on me. This thing had a wide band that reached from just above my hips up to my shoulder blades. Across the front was a padded steel strap that crossed my chest. Attached to this was another strap that ran down my right side to the wide belt band, crossing over with a padded V that set on that narrow pelvic bone and then ran up my left side to the strap that crossed my chest.

The wide belt also had a strap on my left side and two clamps (one at the top and the other along my lower side). On the front strap was a device with a band that was hooked to the belt and, using an Allen wrench, they drew it tight around my body. When Dr. Shull was satisfied he had it right, they locked it with the smallest padlock I ever saw. We still have that lock, but the body brace was discarded after sitting in a closet for several years. I did not want to throw it away as it cost $300.

Thank God this thing had an open front as I gassed up so tight that my stomach stuck right through it. It was then that I understood why they let the hole in my roommate's body cast.

After being placed in the thing I began running a high fever from the infected urinary tract. It got up to 103.7° and I sweated so much that I began to stink, and they would change my bed sheets twice a day, during the day and again during the night. I was on antibiotics and since this did not bring the fever down, they began flushing my bladder with a cold salt water solution. They did this for five days and when the fever began going down changed over to sterile water.

I realize now that I was a lot sicker than both Ida and I thought I was. I say this because she began to question Dr. Shull why she could not take me home and care for me herself, and he became somewhat angry with her. He gave her a pretty good talking-to, telling her that no matter what she said he would not release a man with a broken back running a 104° fever. He said, "You both should be thankful he can still move his legs as it was only luck that he did not paralyze himself with all the action he took before getting to a hospital." That scared both of us.

It was here that I met one of the nicest nurses ever. Her husband was a minister at Henley and that was their home. I was so dumb as to not ask her name and for that I am ashamed because I could have at least sent her a thank you note. She was my night duty nurse. She would come in and change my sheet and give me a cool bath. My prostate was bleeding and I was always a mess. I apologized for smelling so bad and she replied, "You are the one who is suffering and my job is to help you as much as I can."

I cannot say this for my day nurse. Although she was nice, she accidently kicked the urinary bottle from my catheter into a bed post, breaking it (yes, they used glass at that time) and that smelly urine spread all over the floor. My roommate and I had to smell that stink for two hours before the housekeeper came to clean it up. This was on a Sunday and that may have been the reason it took so long.

My roommate by then was a man who had a cyst on his arm that bothered him. His name was Walters and it was his brothers who worked for Clarence laying blocks on our dairy barn. He had two brothers who died from cancer and he lucked out as his cyst was benign then. However, he and another brother did die from cancer later on. That must have run in the family.

My last roommate was an 84-year-old man by the name of Merhoff from Bland, Missouri. He was carrying slop from the kitchen to his hog (we did this same thing years ago) and on stepping on a stick fell and broke his thigh bone about three inches below his hip socket. He came from the Catholic hospital at Washington, Missouri where he had been for two weeks. Since the bone did not knit, he was brought to Memorial to have a pin put in. Again Dr. Leslie was the doctor.

This man was a friendly old guy and every evening his granddaughter would visit with him after work. Sometimes she would drive to Bland and then bring her grandmother along for a visit. To see this old couple together and note his wife's concern almost made me cry because I could see he was going downhill. She was a frail old lady and I'm sure the distance from Bland and back was quite a chore for her. They must have been a well-thought-of couple as his minister (Baptist) came to visit him every day also. One thing I will never forget was that my pastor came to visit me only once, although Father Buchanan from St. Peters came to hear my confession and brought me Communion once a week. I appreciate that. I also appreciate that Mr. Merhoff's minister stopped by my bed and asked if he could say a prayer with me too. I told him he certainly could.

As Mr. Merhoff became sicker, I began to get better. On the 18th day, Ida got to bring me home and on the next day I saw in the newspaper that Mr. Merhoff had died. I felt so sorry for that little old lady as she was now alone. I just hoped that the granddaughter took care of her.

While I was at Memorial I got to see my old schoolmate Barbara Probst as she was a housekeeper with the hospital. I also learned that she rented an apartment from my sister Rose. We got to talk over old times and this helped pass the time away.

Then too I got to see my friend Gwen (Braun) Gevecker who as a child I pushed around playing mail carrier. As a registered nurse she had a job training practical nurses and she would bring them into the room and give them instructions as to how to change the beds of such critical patients as Mr. Merhoff.

At home they moved my bed down into the parlor and I was now up in class. I wore my back brace 24 hours of the day. I can tell Dr. Shull that I did not itch under the thing, but it sure as hell pinched me enough to drive me crazy. After being home about a week I began doing the housework so I at least took that much work from Ida. Yet I could watch out the window while doing the dishes and see her forking silage on the wagon.

Not too long after, I told Ida I was going to help and she said, "You're not," and I said, "I am because my back cannot move." I could use my arms and bend from the hips and here was where I got all the pinches along with having all the skin worn off that little bit of pelvic bone the brace rested on. So we bought new soft washcloths and I used them as pads. When one side got bloody we turned them over. Ida tried washing them but after washing they were kind of prickly and ate the heck out of you. I was also still bleeding from my prostate reaming and that continued for two more months.

Since I was getting better, my bed went back upstairs because, after all, who would want a bed in the "best room"? I told Ida then to unlock me so I could take the thing off and again she said, "You're not," and again I said I would. Being bigger and meaner, I won that argument too by agreeing it would be okay at night but not okay during the daytime so it was in and out. I suppose this was compromising and that is why we got along so well throughout our married life. It was really a relief to not have to sleep in the darn thing, and to prove I was boss too.

Throw in the Towel?

WE WERE HAVING AN EXTREMELY WET WINTER in 1968 and hauling silage was a damn chore. Due to the freezing and thawing, the cows did not want to come into the lot for milking. This was because they were breaking through the frozen ground and skinning their legs. So we cut the fence so they could come in another way.

One day Ida and I learned that too, as while unloading silage for the heifers (from the trench silo on the Kirchhoff farm), the darn wagon broke through and sank down to the tandem axle. When trying to pull it out, the old 85 just sat up on the frozen ground and spun its wheels slinging s--t all over everything. It was decided that Ida walk home and get the 65 and a chain. All we got out of that was a broken chain until old Bud got a bright idea. Anything that could pick up a 12-foot disc should lift a silage wagon front. I lowered the hydraulic lift arms down and tied them to the tongue and raised the 85 so that its front end stuck up in the air and the old boy just walked right out of the mud (shit) hole.

I asked Ida, "Why in the hell didn't you think of that sooner?" To make matters worse I had to be at the doctor's office at two o'clock and, even with both of us rushing, this time the doctor had to wait on me like I had been waiting on him.

I will never forget that winter. Ida and I discussed this a lot and it was agreed that some changes needed to be made or quit, one or the other. When David told us he wanted to work at home the summer of 1969, that helped make our decision—we would go all out.

We focused on two major improvements that we hoped would change everything for the better.

The first was to create more stalls for the cows. We called an agricultural engineer named Hubert Krautmann about the shed over the feed manger and this idea was discarded. Instead we planned to rebuild the old barn into a modern free stall by adding a lean-to on the east side of the barn and another lean-to across the north side of the barn. This would give us stalls for 72 cows. Of course we had to remove all the crap, and that included the old milking stanchions, the hall, and the other stables. Taking all this out required beams to hold up the loft and these beams had posts that matched the four-foot width of the stall. Two eight-foot-wide walkways with a curb on each side had a post set every four feet.

After completion, 18 cows faced south, another 18 faced north, and the remaining faced each other in the center of the barn. These center stalls were last on the list and I had to complete them myself. We then poured two and a half acres of concrete, joining the old slab that we had from before and between it and the barn; to the north to join the shed and with a jog to the milking parlor. We then put a retaining wall from just west of the milk barn south to the south of the barn. This was all done to grade so that there could be no standing water.

The second improvement was to upgrade our water situation. We poured an underground pump house by the pond and had the Rural Electric Administration (REA) put a post, meter, and line for service there. We then laid 800 feet of water line to an electric water heater for the cows in the barn lot. This was placed so that cows could water from both sides as a partition fence had to be there to separate the milked cows from the ones yet to be milked.

After we got the water line in, we poured the section east of the barn beginning with the holding area extension all the way to the south end of the barn. This made it so much easier in keeping the milking parlor clean and an easy way to scrape the lot. We placed the posts for the 60-foot feed auger from the new 60 by 20 foot upright silo that just had been built.

Our silo under construction

    I don't know how the three of us got all that done that summer as we had the silo full and three barns full of hay. Of course we had the help of my friends, the quarry workers, on the evenings after work. They would come for supper and afterward we would put up hay until midnight. All I can say is that Ida must have been as good a boss as she was a worker. Below is a picture of Dave and me on a 12-foot concrete float and Ida with a rake pulling concrete ahead of us.

Dave and me spreading concrete, and Ida using rake

Ted was helping Dr. Townley that summer building fences for college money, and the girls did the milking and cleaned the equipment and milk barn. They must have taken those pictures and did the cooking too. Last but not least was the $24,000 loan from the bank, and this included the silo unloader, feed auger, and silo blower. The whole shebang used up a lot of our savings along with the bank loan.

Converting to Grade A Milk

AFTER ALL THE IMPROVEMENTS it was time to convert to Grade A milk, so next was to get the well okayed.

When we installed the jet water system, our instructions were to go down below the freeze line and cut off the well casing at that depth, as there was included a watertight seal that fit in the casing. This was a two-piece deal with a one-inch-thick rubber gasket and as you screwed down the cap screws, it squeezed the rubber tightly around both pipes and expanded inside the well casing. This was water (ground water) tight. There is no way I can figure why this would not pass the State Department of Health requirements for producing milk. All they would have to do was to test the water and if it tested pure, we should have been in the clear. They would not do this as the well had to meet their specifications. Like my brother Carl said, "college graduates" and all. He produced Grade A milk too.

This is what we had to do. Remember I told you there was a little house and pump shed and it had a concrete floor. Well, we busted out the concrete to put the pump underground and after we put in the new plastic hoses we replaced the concrete and made a welding shed out of it. Now we had to bust out the concrete again and dig down to where we had cut the well casing off and we then had to weld another casing to replace what we had removed, adding another two feet so it stuck above ground. Get this! Since the plastic tubing was now too short on both pipes, we added galvanized pipe for extra length, put on two ells, two nipples, another two ells and ran right back into the ground to connect to the plastic pipes. Then we had to build a box and insulate the pipes so they would not freeze. Now that darn box sat right there in the middle of our welding room.

This isn't all. Since those two plastic pipes from the well to the cellar ran under the sewer, I thought for sure we were going to have to jump them too. To be sure I was getting angry and asked the man why. His answer was the sewer might leak into the water lines and contaminate the water with bacteria. (Never mind that we had been drinking this water all those years and were still there.) I asked him how in the hell could sewage leak into a water line that was under 40 pounds of pressure. He said he "guessed" it could not, so we did not have to put the loop there. Think about this when you drink a glass of milk and consider all the sanitary conditions required to get it to you. No one gets too old to learn a new way of doing something dumb.

Fairs, 4-H, and Future Farmers

DAVID HAD BUILT A WAGON while in FFA and won many awards with it at fairs in Linn, Belle, and the FFA Fair at Windsor as well as at the State and Cole County Fairs. This wagon, along with a new Case, was used to haul lots of wheat after the truck was sold. I would hook both behind the 85 and head those nine miles to market. Both of these wagons were also converted to silage haulers when doing our chopping and custom work. The bad thing was the silage had to be pulled off by a sling pulled by a tractor.

Back row: Ida, me, Beverly. Front row: Ted, Karen, David. Circa 1970s.

All our daughters and sons held every officer position in 4-H, and Karen and Beverly did also in Future Homemakers of America. Well, as the thinking of today goes, that was a great waste of time. Still, we were as proud of them as they were of themselves. This goes for both boys as they were also officers for Future Farmers of America. I'm sure all of them can remember the days of the fairs, sleeping on straw while showing their cows and calves. Seems like all of them came up with Blue Ribbons for 4-H and FFA, but the open show was a little tougher. One time our show cow came in sixth place and while Ted was lining up for awards, another boy slipped his cow ahead of Ted's. Ted then came up seventh and Ida was so angry that I had to hold her to keep trouble down (or was it the other way around?). All our friends sitting with us said, "You should raise hell," but Ted and I were too chicken. Ida as a 4-H leader would have stood in there and fought.

After the livestock show closed on the Saturday evening at the Cole County Fair, Ted stayed with his show trailer and Dave's wagon. We loaded all on the wagon and put Ted's show heifer on the pickup and headed for home. All the rest of us had gone to confession that afternoon and Ted was to stop by St. Martin's Church. It was hot that August evening so they had the old church door open for air. The story goes that all show animals became pets and became attached to the one who groomed them. Well that heifer saw Ted walk into church for confession and mooed and mooed until he came back out. I guess that helped him, as with the heifer's bawling, I'm sure the priest could not hear all those "bad" sins.

Ted, Dave, and I, along with the two Cook sons, went to the FFA Regional Show with their calves along with ours and a young bull we were keeping. (That bull became Mr. Joe.) We hooked Dave's wagon on behind, loaded with loading chutes, trailers, a three-point hookup lifting boom, and show boxes with the needed grooming equipment and spent three whole days there. I was never so sick of sleeping on a truck in my life. We went to Warsaw to see the Truman Dam that they were starting to build and the Cook boys leaned against a light chicken fence put along the edge of a 200-foot-high bluff trying to see more, seemingly unconcerned at the danger of leaning like that. The work crew had just started building the concrete dam part across the river and way out in the river bottom. We did get around, didn't we?

I bet Dave remembers the days when, after we got the new John Deere mower, we would rent a crimper and he would follow me with the little Ferguson 30 crimping because it crushed the stems so the alfalfa would dry quicker and make better hay. One time Anton Prenger hauled all the chicken manure on his bottom field. He sold hatching eggs from about 5,000 hens and that created a hell of a lot of manure. The oats grew as big as trees and lay so thick it would not dry. This was after we got our own crimper and Anton hired Dave to crimp the hay, but he could not because it wrapped around the crimper. This was during the International T-56 Commercial baler days, and the bales were so thick that they fell to the ground one after another with no space between them. I will never forget that field as it completely wore out the little four-cylinder baler motor and we replaced it with a big 32-horsepower Wisconsin air-cooled. Later that baler left for a Ferguson 9 and a larger 14 and even later for a John Deere 336 with a bale thrower. We could then "throw" bales on the silage wagons and did away with pulling a wagon and loader. I could then bale and load myself and keep ahead of the barn unloading help. Seems like when people got smarter, they could always find ways of making things easier to do.

As my help left home, I traded the John Deere mower for one with a hitch and I could mow and crimp at the same time. As people got smarter yet, they combined a mower and a crimper into what was called a "haybine" and of course we got one of those too. All these sorts of things made it easier to get bigger, so we didn't save any work either. Just made it so one man could do more of it.

Ted was accepted into veterinary school at University of Missouri as a junior and came home one Saturday and said he wanted to help me plow. I told him to put the plow on the 65 Massey because the John Deere had the loader on it. Since it was quick-attach, he said he would remove it as he wanted to drive the new tractor. When he got to the field, it overheated on the first round and we learned that the water had gone into the crankcase. Now he had to take the plow off and put it on the 65 anyway. We did plow that day, almost losing the time of Ted's help by changing tractors.

We had purchased this tractor from the Jamestown dealer and he went bankrupt. I had to call the dealer in Tipton. I told him I thought it had a leaking head gasket but he informed me the trouble was much worse than that. He told me it had a loose sleeve (wet sleeve), as when John Deere changed from the old two-cylinder "Johnny Popper" to the four-cylinder engine they had a problem with those sleeves working loose. As in all wet-sleeve motors, the top was sealed by the head gasket and the bottom end by a rubber ring. The problem was that it was not fit tight enough and would work in the block and in our tractor it only took 700 hours to do it.

After I brought the John Deere tractor into the shop, I was first told that all they had to do was pull each sleeve and not disturb the piston and put in an improved Neoprene ring. I was then called and told that John Deere had sent out a bulletin stating that this had not proved successful and that they had designed a new sleeve that would have three steps with a ring on each step. They did not yet have the grinder designed to cut out the motor block to accommodate the new sleeve. That would take about a month. When they brought the tractor back, I used it five hours and the oil pressure light came on so I shut it off. Here I was told that I needed to put a 3/8-inch flat washer behind the oil pressure release and the dealer gave me the washer.

Well, Ida and I had to remove the radiator to do this and it was almost impossible to get the spring compressed to start the threads. I still had no oil pressure. I went back again and this time was told to install a new oil filter as they were full-flow. After doing this we still had no luck. By this time I was angry because I felt we were getting the runaround and told them to come down and get the thing. To make matters worse, this was on a $14,000 tractor and it was already in their shop for two months. They and John Deere would not believe me and put it on a dynamometer and ran it under load and just ate the motor up.

In the meantime, I was planting corn with the 65 on the planter, running it in low range as the multi-power had begun slipping. The 85 was pulling a 12-foot disc along with a 14-foot drag harrow. Be assured I was working my butt off trying to get the corn planted and was interrupted by the smartest (he thought so) John Deere field man and fuzz began to fly.

He said, "Do you still have the oil filter we told you to remove?" and I said, "Yes," as there was nothing wrong with it and I thought to save five dollars. He said, "We want to run an analysis, because you sent your oil up here and we think the two jugs you used had grit in them." I told him, "Look fellow, that tractor was mine and why should I send oil up to ruin it? Besides, I use those jugs each time I change oil in all of my equipment and there are two Masseys running now while that damn John Deere has been at your dealer's shop." At this time another two months had passed with still no tractor.

His answer was, "Mr. Mertens, I would watch them close as you may have somebody trying to get even with you."

I told him we had lived here for over 15 years with no problems and now it is time to talk. I said, "You had better look around at all the green machinery I have here and then go back and get my tractor back."

Well I did get it back with a ground-down crankshaft and I hit the ceiling again. Mr. Shafter the dealer (what a name for a dealer who sold, among other things, crankshafts!) said it almost took an act of Congress to get John Deere to do that much. He called me later and said, "You are unhappy with that tractor, aren't you?"

I told him, "Who wouldn't be? A new tractor with a ground down crankshaft."

This was a gas tractor so he said he would trade me a new 2020 diesel if I would pay the difference between the gas and diesel which was at that time $2,500 as he said they did not have any problems with the diesel motor. Since it was not the dealer's fault, Ida and I thought it over for three days and then made the change. Oh well! Just a few more debts.

I end this chapter at the age of 52, December 20, 1969 and Ida just one month after beginning her 46th year. Thank God for those 24 years of so much love.

The Last of Our Dairy Cattle Years

Earning Degrees and Winning Awards

WE STARTED THE YEAR of 1970 with the good news that David, after completing his Masters at the University of Missouri, was recruited to attend Cornell University at Ithica, New York. He was to be a teaching assistant while working toward his Ph.D. This would support him while studying under the renowned scientist Dr. Peter Van Sooest. It was then that Ralston-Purina granted him a $4,000 scholarship so he had to surrender his teaching assistantship to another student in need. He wondered what he would have to do the next year but Ralston followed through with another scholarship to the amount of $4,600. So he had the money to complete his Doctors of Philosophy in Animal Nutrition.

Missouri State Farm Management Award

For us here, we won the Missouri State Farm Management Award for the western half of Missouri. We were one of 12 farm families to receive this award. Ours was for agricultural economics and the others were one each in specialties such as beef, hogs, sheep, agronomy, etc.

We were invited by the Greater Chamber of Commerce of Kansas City, Missouri to the Muhlebach Hotel for lunch and the awards were to be presented by the Chamber. This made for one hell of a rush for Ida and me. We had to first milk the cows and then meet our county extension agent in California at half past eight o'clock. Be assured we got an early start to get everything cleaned up so we had a very early breakfast. Of course we were supposed to be at the hotel in Kansas City early enough for the coffee and doughnuts and to get acquainted with each other while eating those doughnuts. Well it did not work out that way for the Mertens or the Rileys, as when we each arrived that part was already over. Seems a bit strange they thought farming folk could get to such an event so early—didn't they know how much work went into farming each day?

What we did get to do was listen to a welcoming speech by the mayor and speeches by some city council members and of course by the president of the Chamber of Commerce. It was then time for our "starving to death" meal. They placed five of us to a table. At ours were Mr. and Mrs. William Riley (our extension agent for Moniteau County), Ida and me, and a member of the Chamber of Commerce. I'm sure the man was embarrassed about the meal. Each of us was served with a covered silver platter and it stayed covered until all the tables were served. Then the waiters went to each table and removed the covers and we were shocked.

Our meal consisted of a small slice of cooked beef, a small portion of beef noodles, a tablespoonful of whole kernel corn and a biscuit so hard we thought we may have to put it on the floor and stomp it to pieces. Our dessert was a goblet of custard. It was served in a dish like one of those in which St. Mary's Hospital served their soft-boiled eggs. After the meal, we received a plaque and a "build up" talk about how wonderful we farmers were and how much Kansas City benefitted from our hard work as it was a town that depended on the farm families. We got much more out of the writeup the newspapers gave us. We still have those newspaper clippings.

Newspaper article about our farm management award

As a result of the writeups, we received a nice letter of praise from Uncle Jake and Aunt Lena Kolb and a phone call from Bernard and Kenneth Mertens congratulating us after they read about it while working on a construction job near Warrenton, Missouri.

It was also in 1970 that Ted, as a junior in college, was accepted into veterinary school. This cut his eight years of college to seven and of course that was also a great help. One year less for college expense.

Karen did not want to go to college, although they tried very hard to recruit her. She took a job with the Missouri State Department of Revenue and remained with that department until she married.

The year of 1971 saw some upgrading of our machinery. The old 85 Massey left for a 6606 Deutz Diesel. Later the 65 was traded for a 175, a more powerful Massey tractor. We now had two tractors that could handle the field chopper while also pulling the wagon. My brother Emil began working for us, arriving in the morning and going home in the evening. We had reached the stage where Ida, Bev, and I could not do all the work, although Karen helped with the calves before and after work. Since Bev planned on going to college, it was also necessary for her to begin working in the office for M.F.A. (Missouri Farmers Association) as did Ted who worked in the grain end.

The 40 combine was traded for a 45 John Deere, equipped with 18.4 by 28 "rice" tires and single-rib rear tires of 7.50 by 16. I'm telling you this as this combine gave me one hell of a scare as I will relate to you later on.

For silage corn we rented the Moreau River bottom from our neighbor Bruce Cook. It was 45 acres and had started to grow Johnson grass, a difficult-to-control weed grass. He wanted it removed before the grass went to seed and this fit in good for silage. It was a long haul and it took all 45 acres to fill the new upright silo. Emil really enjoyed driving the Deutz (German made and air cooled) as it was ahead of American makes in that it had a synchronized transmission. It also had an accelerator (foot gas-feed that could also be set at the desired speed if wanted). There was a steep hill from the bottom and the Deutz had the needed weight over the 175 Massey to pull six tons of silage up it. There were many ups and downs on the road so Emil just drove that tractor like driving his truck, although he too had quit lime and phosphate hauling.

Emil's beer drinking had evolved to include other liquors. It was the beginning of a problem. It had gotten so that I was afraid he would hurt himself so I had to ask him to either quit drinking or quit working for us. He did not so we were again without help. (In later years he was forced to quit and I'm proud to say that he did.)

Again sadness came to the family as Ida's dad died suddenly from an aneurysm. We were all home for a great Christmas and he had so much fun with his many grandchildren, yet he was dead only four days later on December 29, 1971. He was 75 years of age.

David Meets Carolyn

IN 1971 DAVID BROKE HIS LEG while skiing and had many X-rays. Through these he met the technician Carolyn Ann Miller and fell in love with her. Carolyn is of Polish descent and her Polish name was changed when her grandfather emigrated to America. The name is Przydryga and the emigration officer admitting him could not pronounce it. So he declared, "Your name from now on will be Miller."

So it became time for the Mertens to meet Carolyn and that meant a trip to New York. This worked out well since Karen and Bev, with weekend help from Ted, would take care of the farm. We left on a Thursday morning, hoping everything worked out okay, and made it to just north of Columbus, Ohio that day. I can't think of the town's name right now but we were tired. Ida had fixed us sandwiches so we only stopped at rest stops to eat and relieve ourselves. There were some pressed ham sandwiches left over and before going to bed I ate them. They must have become spoiled as I really got sick. It brought back memories of the ham sandwiches from my bachelor party that nearly ruined my wedding day but this time I could vomit and I think that helped although I had a pretty weak stomach at breakfast time.

We took off early in the morning because we wanted to visit Niagara Falls since we would be so close to them. We were driving the old 1967 Plymouth with just over 49,000 miles on it when at Niagara we began to hear a noise. We'd heard this same noise once before. It sounded to be a front wheel bearing, the dealer had thought, and he replaced it under warranty. We took it to the Chrysler garage in Niagara Falls, New York and were told that they were union and were closing in five minutes (half past four o'clock) and that we would have to lay over until morning. I told him we were supposed to be in Ithica by six o'clock and could not wait as we were expected there for a great meal of duck. He told me to wait a few minutes and he would get back to me. We did this and when the shop closed he told me he had another place to do warranty work but could not let the union know about it.

We took the car to this place and the man worked hard, pulling all the wheels to check the bearings and could find nothing wrong. We went for another test drive and the noise still pointed to the right front wheel. He then took the drive line down to check the universal joints although when those go bad there is always a hell of a vibration and we did not have that. Again he found nothing wrong so another test drive. This time he practically hung outside the car through the window and said, "Let's go back as it has to be the right front wheel." As we were driving along he said, "Would you mind if I disconnect the speedometer cable?" We stopped and he got underneath and did that and found the darn noise. When we got back to his garage he took out the cable and oiled it.

We got to visit the American Falls but did not have time to visit the Canadian ones, which are the best. We did see them many years later.

When I look back, I think about how a minor thing such as we had could scare the hell out of you just because you are 1,000 miles away from home. Since the old car had a 50,000-mile warranty, it cost Chrysler two repair jobs and a wheel bearing that was not needed in the first place. One thing I can say is that neither Ida nor I had ever met before such a nice man as the guy who did that work.

We reached Ithica in time for a late duck supper and met our future daughter-in-law. Remember we left on a Thursday and took all day Friday to get there. So, since we had to be back to milk cows on Monday, that meant we had to start on Saturday morning for the two-day trip back.

Everyone who drinks a glass of milk should understand that to be a dairyman is a 16-hours-a-day, 365-days-a-year job. There was no vacation for us during those 28 years and anything we would have enjoyed was cut short like the trip to New York. I am sure we were considered by the Stockman family, when we had our get-togethers, as nutty because we would arrive for dinner only to find it ready at about the time we had to go back home to milk. Well! Maybe we got the last laugh as I'm sure Ida and I can now buy any of them out if we care to.

Quality Over Quantity

THAT SUMMER Beverly began college so we were even more short of help. We also began to accept city-to-farm tours and had three of them. Then too, Professor Albert Baker would bring two buses of Ag-Econ students to visit the farm they were working with. We were compared to a 3,000-acre ranch and, as I remember, it was hill land at Camdenton, Missouri and suitable only for beef in their regard. It was of the same type of land as we had. Professor Baker would ask the students why we had more return on investment than that ranch, which as they thought, was making the most returns.

It was on one of those visits that I almost fell out with our extension agent from the University of Missouri. He made this remark to the students and I quote: "Mr. Mertens had this silo built against my advice and thereby brought his investment returns from 10% down to just above 8%. Now if he had kept the old trench silos, he could have kept those high returns." I told the students that I could depreciate the $18,000 cost over 18 years so that would be $1,000 per year and at our age, if we could not make it easier on ourselves, we may as well quit. That surely we were entitled to the convenience of the ease of feeding and that a thousand dollars per year would in no way equal the cost of hiring a man. I also told them that we thought the better quality of the silage would in itself make up the cost in milk production at a later date. This was so true as our dairy herd proved.

Since we now had quality feed and were testing for protein and energy, we began to disagree with our grain supplier, Ralston-Purina. It seemed they always wanted to substitute quality of feed to hold cost down as they said.

Like milo instead of corn. Both may have the same energy basis but we knew that milo was not as palatable as corn, nor was cottonseed cake or rapeseed meal as palatable as soybean meal. It seemed to always be an argument, so we decided to purchase a John Deere mixer-grinder and grind our feed as we wanted. To keep milk production up you always treated your cows better than yourselves.

Ida weighing feed

When we fed corn silage along with a lesser amount of alfalfa, we always increased the energy in the feed and when we fed haylage, since it usually tested to be 17% to 20% protein, we would decrease the soybean meal. Corn silage, if it were tops, might get up to 8% protein so we used urea (ammonium nitrate) in the amount of a 50-pound bag to one ton of silage as we blew it into the silo. Urea, too, was unpalatable so we held ours down to one bag per ton instead of two as recommended. Our veterinarian was against adding the urea as his feeling was that it lowered the reproduction rate of the cow. We cut the urea (derived from mammalian urine) to one half as I said. We stayed with that rate as we had a very good calving rate of 324 days lactation average so we had our cows calving 384 days with a two-month dry period to get back into high production.

Of course other dairymen didn't always agree with the way we handled our cows. We sorted our cows as they entered the milking parlor so the first-calf heifers were first and the clean cows second. Any cow that at any time had mastitis and was cured came next and those with mastitis currently were milked last. In this way we held down the spread of disease.

Many dairymen wanted to get out of the milk barn as soon as possible, bragging that they could milk 100 cows an hour. We did not even try to be the fastest as our cows were making us our livelihood so we let our cows eat the amount of dairy ration according to their production. For example, a cow that gave 90 pounds of milk was entitled to eat her ration of over 32 pounds of feed. This was nice and we could do this as our milk parlor was a bypass arrangement so the high-producing cow could continue to eat while one at the end of her lactation could be turned away sooner since she had less feed and another cow could enter in her place.

So instead of 100 cows per hour we used two hours for the 60 to 80 we milked. It took more time to sort the cows and to feed in the barn according to production. We spent more time in the milk parlor but came away proud because we had a low somatic cell and bacteria count and as such got called upon to give many speeches in the St. Louis shed so that other dairymen could benefit from our method if they cared to. Today milk is paid for according to quality, with a 20% premium for top quality, regular price for normal, and a 20% discount for low quality. How we would have loved that pricing system in our days of milking as we were in the top bracket. We are proud of this because both our milk inspector and veterinarian spoke to the buyers at our sale in 1974 when we quit the dairy farm business and read our calving interval and somatic and bacteria count. This helped our cows sell at prices well beyond our expectations.

We had a good reputation as we hosted city tours so people could see our operation. We also had a group of five men from India who came to view the way we milked to take ideas back to India to better their production. Many times I wondered which they chose: our style or the 100-cow-per-hour man. To me, since they had such a high population in their country, maybe they chose, or should have chosen, our way as they certainly had the manpower to do it the slow way.

Newspaper article about our farm tours

To talk with these people we had to go through an interpreter. I would think that they learned more by seeing than by what was translated to them. We also hosted two English teachers from Brazil for a long weekend. We had no problem there as they could speak English better than we could. Both of these girls were Catholics and were surprised to see so many of us Catholics at Sunday Mass. In their country it was mostly a Holy Day thing. They were touring our country to learn our way of teaching English.

So many things were taking place in the year of 1971. One of them could have been a disaster. Before Beverly began college, she and Karen would get the cows home for morning milking while Ida made breakfast and I rinsed the milker and got it in the parlor for milking. That morning Ida called them from sleep to get the cows but they were slow in getting started and a bad storm was approaching. Ida told them to wait until it passed over and there were several close lightning strikes nearby. When they got to the cows they found that four had been killed and they could have been right there if Ida had let them go sooner. Three of these were our better cows and were standing near a fence that the lightning hit quite a ways away and ran through the wire to where the cows were standing. This was more than a $3,000 loss to us according to what the cows sold for later. The insurance only paid market value for beef and that was our loss. Be assured we then changed companies to one that would pay the value for production. We only lost one other cow later by lightning and that cow was not more than 400 feet from where Ida and I were unloading feed into a calf feeder. We did receive production value for her. When we think about it, we have to admit God was with us in many ways—the girls had been safe inside, and also with the great number of cows we owned we only lost five by lightning.

After Bev began college it was my job to get the cows while Ida put the equipment together. While I walked, I began to feel for the kids as I never did so much stumbling around while walking with a flashlight. Seems like there was always a high or low spot to fall over.

When the girls had to go after the cows, they wanted a horse. Knowing a horse had no place with dairy cattle I bought one of the first three-wheel Hondas sold here. I remember the time it gave Beverly an unexpected thrill by dumping her into the creek and she came home all wet. This thing became the work horse for the family and me. Gave $550 for the three-wheeler and after Dave and Ted tried to tear it apart by jumping it over terrace berms, sold it on our machinery sale for $960. I bet they remember when they jumped the drive chain off when it hit the ground and I had to take it all apart to get the chain from between the gears. Darn those boys anyhow! This thing was real good for getting cows in the morning and when it was dark. It had a strong headlight and you could use that beam to find the cows. It was a real money-maker for us. Not only did it sell high on our sale, it also became a part of a class action lawsuit against Honda because another buyer found that Honda sold 1971 models as 1972. Got a letter from New York from the First District of Federal Court. Well, Honda lost the suit and thus we received a check for $45 for our share and didn't have to do a thing to get it. What a gift.

I want to get more about dairying into the story as some readers may be thinking of becoming dairymen. That is if you like lots of work.

Right! No way for that because I'm sure none of you would be so foolish. My advice is to continue drinking milk produced by another.

One time we went on a dairy tour to a farm owned by Ida's cousin Louis Mehmert, Jr. to note how he handled manure to meet a point source of water contamination regulation as we had that coming up too. Louis farmed up from Chamois, Missouri and his son is still dairying there.

He had a different way of feeding his cows as he was one of those fast-milking men. He hardly fed any feed while milking. So to get feed into the better producers he had a dividing gate. This was so he could put his better producers to a self-feeder. Each cow there could eat as much as they wanted and many times a lower producer could keep a high producer from getting her share accordingly. You can bet he was questioned on this and his reply was, "If one of my cows gets fat she goes to market as she is not putting the extra into milk."

To me this was a poor way of thinking as many things can make your best producer become fat. One of those is too much energy (corn) in your ration. This was the main reason we tested our feed but he said he was too busy for that sort of thing. Second he was overfeeding some of his cows that did not milk as high as some others and then selling them for market price when his idea of feeding was the cause of the fat. Of course he did not have to work at it as we did because he was also a rural mail carrier. But some people prefer quantity over quality and that is not us.

Getting Wired

THE SAYING GOES that there is no rest for the wicked and we surely were tops in that regard because we always had the work even if it took electrical outages to do it. We were members of REA Co-Mo Electrical Cooperative and they gave very good service until someone shot an insulator and they could not find which one it was. So it came about that we lost electricity during about three days of rain and Ida and I had to milk the cows by hand. Milking was not a two-hour job then. It was continuous throughout the day. Our thumbs and wrists hurt so much we could almost cry but knowing that would not help we just had to keep on.

To make matters worse we, without thinking, placed the warm milk in the bulk tank and with no cooling the milk truck driver did not pick up the milk. We called the Mid-America field man and asked what to do. He was an elderly man and a gem of a guy. He came to our home and took a sample to test but while we were talking he drank it. Then he took another sample and drank that one too and said, "There is nothing wrong with the milk," and called the trucker and told him to pick it up. We lucked out as we are talking about $430 worth of milk.

We learned that we had to be prepared for this sort of thing so we decided to buy an alternator for our own electrical service. We called in REA and they came down and decided that, since the farm was wired for the $1.40 per month rate instead of the $4.00 rate, we did not have a large enough transformer and entrance wiring. They said they didn't know how we were getting by as, along with the farm and home electrical use, we had added 42 horsepower of motors. The odd thing about this was that while we were "getting by" we did have problems with one motor and that one was the two-horsepower motor on the milking machine. Here we would call the DeLaval dealer and he would put a new motor on it under warranty, blaming the motor. He replaced three of them.

REA decided we needed a 75 kW transformer and a much heavier wire to the meter pole. Since we planned on the alternator they suggested it be of the same size as the transformer rating. They would do their part for nothing as we were members but told us that we had to install a cutoff switch box that would disconnect the highline while we were using the alternator.

We wanted to mount the alternator on a trailer, that we could also mount our welder on, so that we could put it under cover when not in use. Here we were advised to get a Gen-Arc brand as they used two alternators running opposed to each other to generate 75 kW. Other makes of this size would have to be mounted on a concrete block to keep them from spinning around when you threw 20 horsepower of motors on them. It would make the 75-horsepower tractors shoot out black smoke when you turned the silo on. We soon learned to turn on one motor at a time as the large one made both the trailer and tractor bounce.

By the time they got this all installed, the mail carrier saw a highline pole on fire and then they found the damaged insulator. In fact, at first we only used the alternator to do field welding and while welding on the combine David and I set the wheat field on fire and fought like hell with our feet stomping the fire out. Believe me we both had hot shoes.

Later on we had two ice storms, one of three days length, and it was then that the alternator was used steady 24 hours of the day. That was necessary to keep the bulk tank cooling. We could watch television and one evening Bev thought to be funny and called her friend and asked her if she was watching the good TV show. Here they were on their farm using kerosene lamps and thought Bev was kidding.

Getting Prettier

WE ARE IN 1972 NOW and the Environmental Manure Handling System we were required to build. Clarence backed away from this job as it required much excavation so we hired Frank Distler of Jefferson City to do the work. He was a building contractor who, at the time many Veit boys were attending St. Peters High School, took care of the buildings for St. Peters Parish. This got him into the construction business. When he finished the manure pit, we had him put new ceilings in the TV room and the living room. He also put in new concrete back steps to replace those that were going bad.

Our farm home was of unusual design in that it had both an upper and lower front porch. The railing on the upper one had gone bad so we took the door knob away so the kids could not get on it and fall off. Both of those porches were of wood and were going bad. Ida wanted a concrete porch with a steel railing and steps that entered upon it from the south side. The upper door was replaced by a window and the top porch completely removed with two pillars reaching to the roof. Now we had a home that looked southern like a plantation but we were not in that class yet. We were still trying to fool ourselves.

The old sidewalk that ran to the road was torn up and a new one that ran south toward the lot was put in. Now we had a sidewalk that allowed people to park and still come in the front door as they were supposed to in the first place. Remember? The complete job cost $4,200. I could say we were just a little prettier maybe. We thought so at least. By the way, our daughter had an amateur artist paint our home from a picture taken during the winter with snow on the ground. He changed this to summertime and had leaves on the trees and it is beautiful. He worked for the Conservation Commission, where Bev works. He later borrowed the painting and took it to Chicago and won an award. Come see it some time.

Award-winning painting of house

David Marries Carolyn

THIS WAS ALSO THE YEAR that David married Carolyn Ann Miller, a pretty young lady from Elmira, New York. Elmira is noted as the burial place of Mark Twain, which is interesting as Florida, Missouri is the birthplace of Mark Twain and that's not even a two-hour drive from us. Elmira is also home of the great American LaFrance Fire Truck. I put new tires on two of such trucks in 1947 for the Jefferson City Fire Department. Sadly, this truck is no longer built, if I remember right.

The decision was made that before we made this high-speed trip to New York for the wedding, we would drive a new car. So we got a 1972 Plymouth which had, for us, the new features of cruise control and a fancy deal that turned out the headlights if older people forgot to. Also, one button would lock all the doors and that fit right in with New York state. Beverly had to show this new car to her neighbor friend. On the way there she saw a new home under construction and gave it the eye. When she looked back at the road, she saw that they had dug across the road for a water line and had covered it with about one foot of loose gravel, making a hump. She hit the brakes and that loose gravel caused her to ditch the car. She came up with a bent fender since it was bolted to the bumper. The car had only 28 miles on it. What a stupid thing to do, to fasten a fender to a bumper, and I will include the girl too. That made me an angry old man.

Again we had another race at 80 miles an hour, but at least we could set the cruise control so we did not have to watch the speedometer while driving. All the signs said, "We arrest all speeders," but the law said 80 was it. To be sure, this trip was planned to the minute and almost down to seconds. Also, this time Grandma and the two daughters went along. Poor Ted had all the farm work to do himself and had to skip one day of vet school to do it. So he came home after school on Thursday evening and did the milking. At about that time we were in Terre Haute, Indiana and from there called home to see if he had made it. If he had not, we would have to return home and do a very late milking. He made it so we continued on to our stopping town north of Columbus, Ohio. Here we reserved rooms for the return trip as we would arrive there on our return at about midnight.

David and Carolyn were married in the Catholic Church in Ithica. For attendants Carolyn chose her sister-in-law and David his friend Richard Sappington of California, Missouri.

Dave and Carolyn's wedding photo

Ida's sister Alice and her husband J.B. DeWesplore came up for the weekend to help Ted and do the cooking. After milking, Ted went back to school on Sunday evening and J.B. and Alice held the fort down until we arrived home. J.B. remarked that our house was the first place he slept in where the bed was so hard he got out of it and slept on the floor.

Well that hard mattress was Ida's idea as it was supposed to be better for your back to sleep on a firm mattress and we still do. Those mattresses are so firm that when the kids come home for a visit, they complain too so Ida put a foam mattress that came out of one of our travel trailers over it. We still use the firm one because we are tough and used to it. Now if you come for a visit you can sleep on the one with the foam!

By the way this was also the year that they had the great floods in New York and Pennsylvania that ruined the Corning glass museum in Corning, New York and did so much damage to Carolyn's town of Elmira. This year (1993) it is our turn for floods.

After receiving his Ph.D. from Cornell, David accepted a teaching position with Iowa State University at Ames, Iowa. David and Carolyn purchased an older home there and were living there when our first grandchild, Christa, was born.

Goodbye, Dairy Farming

WE WERE REACHING THE POINT where we could no longer do the dairy farming work. So with just over $47,000 in debts we decided we should disperse our dairy herd and go into the cow and calf beef business along with crop farming. As if that was a cake walk!

We offered our herd in 1973 on private treaty to a dairyman from Columbia and another from Kingdom City (to split between them) for the price of $54,000 as this would make us debt-free and also give us enough money to go into the beef business. They thought we were too high and asked if we were going to have a dispersal sale if we could not sell by private treaty and we said we would. Their answer to this was to wait and buy the cows cheaper on that sale. We worried but our decision was to take that chance.

As 1974 began we got ready for the sale by contacting the noted Holstein dairy auctioneer, Donald J. Bowman, of Auctioneer and Sales Management of Hamilton, Missouri. The assistant auctioneer was Bill Bredemeier of Seneca, Kansas. They agreed to do the sale, the advertising, and mailing of the pedigrees to the Missouri and outstate dairymen. We were to write the pedigree on each animal, furnish the production records, calving interval, and breeding dates. All cows were to be certified to be healthy, tested for pregnancy whether bred or open, and to be guaranteed. They would furnish sale bills that we would distribute locally. The sales commission was to be 10% of the gross sale. This included advertising, printing, and mailing out the sales catalog. They recommended that we hire a noted Holstein breeder to read the pedigrees and make comments about production and calving records.

This would cost us an extra $250 for his day's work. Karen and I would work the sale ring to keep the cows moving while they were being sold. The sale date was Friday, March 29, 1974 beginning at 11 o'clock. The sale bill read:

Clerks: Helen Bowman and Sharon Bredemeier
Ringmen: Tom Oliver, Mike Robertson, Bill Kramer, and Gary Robertson
Pedigrees: Ronald Silverthorn, Bois D'Arc, Missouri
DHIA Tester: John Veit, Route 4, Jefferson City, Missouri
Milk Sales: To Central Dairy, Jefferson City, Missouri – through Mid-America Dairymen
Milk Inspector: O. J. Ely, Jefferson City, Missouri
Milk Hauler: Opie Milk Haulers Inc., Eldon, Missouri
Veterinarian: Dr. M. M. Townley, Jefferson City, Missouri
N.O.B.A. and Mid-West Technician: C.T. and David Mertens
Milk Fieldman: John Rainy, Jefferson City, Missouri
Extension Dairyman: Don R. Day, Linn, Missouri
Terms: Cash – No property removed until settled for
Trucks and dairy insurance available.
Not responsible for accidents.
Any of the above may be contacted for herd information.
Herd can be visited for inspection prior to sale upon family contact between the hours of 11:00 a.m. and 2:00 p.m. No other visits allowed.

When the sale day came, I was somewhat surprised at the small number of people. I had thought the sale tent would be full but to me, wanting all the dollars, it looked like there were not enough people in attendance to have a great sale. Mr. Bowman told me that there never were, and as the people who were there were dairymen, we did not want a lot of onlookers standing around.

I had picked out the better cows to be sold first as I had thought that would set the sale price. Here again I was told I was wrong because a good sale was conducted by the ringmen and that by neck chain numbers, taking in consideration the quality of udders and conformation, the cows would be mixed to sell. What I learned was that a good cow may sell and then a baby calf; a not-so-good cow after a good one. It would be up to the man reading the pedigrees and Karen and me explaining the milking time (slow or fast), whether the cow was calm or flighty, a pet or a show cow or calf.

Advertisement for the sale

You would be surprised how fast the sale progressed. After the sale was over, I thought we made a mistake in selling the equipment last. It was my thinking that most of the equipment would go locally and that many of those buyers would have to leave to do their milking. We sold the alternator, bulk tank, milking machine, pipeline, and the metering feeders. The milker only brought $330 for a $4,000 outfit. The self-filling automatic feeders brought only $225 and their cost was over $1,400. I really believe that, if we had let them stay with the farm, they would have increased the farm value more when we offered it at a later date. That left $3,195 for the bulk tank and alternator with the expensive bulk tank selling for less than the alternator. I think this was because most cow buyers already had the equipment and were not in the market for them.

Our 110 cows and calves went to buyers in Iowa, Illinois, Kansas, Texas, and Arkansas as well as Missouri. We were proud of our cows and almost cried when they left after bringing us the wonderful amount of $82,600. What hurt was, even after capital gains, the IRS and Missouri walked away with over $13,600 of the amount of the sale in income tax. The total for the equipment and cows was $86,350.

Of course Mr. Donald Bowman also got his $8,600 commission, but I feel that doing the sale through him still made us more than if we had it done through a local auctioneer. I also feel that Ronald Silverton earned his $250 for his day of work. Even after paying the sale cost, we came out with $77,500 and that was a good amount over what we had priced the cows by private treaty. Believe me, Mr. Bowman used this fact later when advertising for conducting sales.

The beauty of this sale was that we could pay all of our debts and have money ahead. This we did and thereby had no more financial worries. Dr. Townley, our veterinarian, rented our pasture for the summer so we planned our first vacation, leaving the two daughters to hold down the fort. This was to be a three-week vacation heading for the state of California.

The Freedom to Travel

TED GRADUATED from vet school that June and took a job and future partnership in the state of Wisconsin. Ida and I thought of purchasing a motor home but when Ted purchased a new half-ton pickup she got the idea of why not buy a heavy pickup and a self-contained slide-in camper. Remember this was in 1974, the year of the oil embargo and the service station lines. Karen also wanted to trade her car, a 1962 Plymouth, for a new one so the three of us headed for the Dodge dealer, knowing that with only one trade-in for Karen's car we could get a great deal.

Ted got his Dodge pickup and Karen got a new Plymouth Satellite Sebring (a car in the class of an Oldsmobile 442, only she got an automatic). I am telling you about this car, as shortly after she had purchased it, we had a severe windstorm. Ted had his car parked ahead of hers and when he left she, for some reason, moved her car up into that place. This was of the love of God as we had a beautiful hard maple (red foliage in the fall) with a fork about 12 feet up the trunk. That windstorm split the tree by the fork and it fell exactly where she had moved her car from. Some of the smaller limbs hit the car but did no damage. Remember that, Karen? How lucky you were.

We then loaded Ted's furniture on our pickup with Ida driving Ted's pickup with the new vet bed he had installed and he driving his car because his mother refused to due to its four-speed close-shifting transmission. (She and I would get it and Dave's car in reverse instead of second.) After we got Ted settled into his apartment in Wisconsin, we headed for home. It was then that we purchased a 12 1/2 foot, slide-in camper and headed on our vacation.

After sightseeing at the Alamo and other places along the way we made it to Del Rio, Texas for three days with our niece Lydia and her husband Lee who was in the Border Patrol. In fact, he was the supervisor and later was transferred to the U.S. Immigration Service. We did not get to visit Mexico while there as Lee advised us not to take the camper into Mexico. He said they would tear it to pieces looking for drugs when we came back to the States. We spent our days with them on their cabin cruiser touring Lake Amistad (on the Rio Grande River), a joint lake with Mexico. When leaving there we headed west and to the Big Bend National Park. I am including this in my story because a scary (so far as Ida was concerned) incident took place.

Here goes. On the way there we went through Geronimo Country, the Chihuahua Mountain area where Geronimo hid out during his raiding. This was on U.S. Highway 385 just at the point of entering Big Bend and we had planned on camping in the Big Bend Basin. I have no idea if this was a prehistoric volcano but it was a huge basin with mountains all around it. This is a beautiful area to visit as there are hiking and horseback riding trails.

Big Bend Basin

As we entered into the basin a sign said, "Stop. Put your vehicle into low gear and then proceed." This in itself scared Ida as she thought we would not make it back out. We did make it out and when we were leaving a park ranger asked, "Where are you heading?"

We told him our next overnight stop would be Tombstone, Arizona.

He said, "I can save you many miles if you do not care about traveling on unpaved roads and I will draw you a map." He also said there would be dry washes on the road and if there was any water in them it would be from a flash flood so to be careful. This also had Ida sitting on the edge of the seat. This route was along the Rio Grande River and there would be many picturesque sights. The painted desert of Texas was the best of all.

The paved road would end at Candleland, Texas and then we were to use a desert road to Texas 192 about 20 miles south of Interstate 10 and we could get on Interstate 10 at McNary, Texas. It would be a good day's drive to Tombstone. The ranger drew up a route on a piece of paper and said there was only one way to get off the desert road and that was at a tree by a ghost town. Here we were supposed to turn left.

After touring the ghost town, we decided that he must have meant turn right as to turn left would head us back in the direction where we came from. You can't believe this, but after driving many hours and miles we made the largest damn circle and came right where we entered the unpaved road.

"What if we have trouble?" Ida asked, while we were driving on that road.

I replied, "We have enough food and water for three days and surely someone would come by in that time."

I was not sure myself as we met only one pickup and it sure was beat up. I don't know how, but some way we got back to U.S. 90 at Marie, Texas and with the luck of God found a service station. This station sat off the road and we had to cross a cattle guard to get to it. I'm saying this because just before we got there we used up a tank of gas and when I switched to the full tank the pickup would not go faster than 20 miles an hour. We limped to that station and made it to Deming, New Mexico at about 10 o'clock at night and camped in a campground just beside a trucking terminal on a grade. Trucks came and went all night long and how in the hell could we get any sleep.

I can tell you this, if you want to live to an old age do not get lost in the desert when you have your wife along. It just isn't safe. We were now behind so we passed right on by Tombstone and wound up the next night at Phoenix, Arizona and got a set of tools to clean out a gas line. Don't tell anyone I said this. I wound up a hell of a lot smarter and never again in all of our travels did we get off a paved road. Just don't give me the credit. Ida wouldn't let me.

From Cattle to Retirement

Where's the Beef?

BEGINNING IN THE YEAR OF 1975 we became beef feeder/calf producers. We purchased many Angus cows to supplement the Holstein-Angus cross from our lower-producing cows. (This was recommended to us since they would be extremely good milking mothers.) These we kept at the home farm.

We stopped buying when we had a total of 40 and purchased a performance-tested Hereford bull from Renn at Elston. He cost $900 and he was a rogue. We had a hell of a time in keeping him at home. The idea was to produce a cross-breed that were called black baldies since they were black with a white face. This bull was polled (no horns) and we knocked them off of the calves. In 1975 calves were selling for $.70 per pound.

On the other farms we placed 40 head of whiteface (Hereford) cows and purchased a weight-gain-rate performance-tested Angus bull at a Fayette, Missouri Angus sale. Such a bull is supposed to pass his weight-gain-rate performance on to his progeny. This one cost us $1,000. He stayed at home but we had another problem.

To prove a good weight gain rate, a young bull was fed accordingly even to the point of not weaning him. So here we found that we had a two-year-old bull that was still sucking his mother or another. We had a hell of a time breaking him of that. He would aggravate a cow until she would finally stand and thus he would take milk away from the calf. To break him of this we had to place a spiked ring in his nose and the poor cow was the one who suffered. Be assured she did not stand for that thing.

Angus bull [8]

Our second problem was that when purchasing cows with calves, we paid over $300 per pair. The calves, when they were ready to sell that fall, were down to $.42 per pound and the next year cows were down to $150. So after our first year as beef people we noted when filing income tax that we lost $29. What a come-down from those milk cows.

Kicked by a Cow

IDA IS NOT ACCIDENT-PRONE like me. The only time she has ever been in a hospital was for the birth of our children and lately as an outpatient for mammograms. She's tough. There was one time I thought I was going to lose her though.

We were sorting beef cows one morning to change bulls. We were working the cows away one at a time while the bull was penned between the auger feeder and the barn so we thought we were fine. We were also removing some young heifers that we wanted to keep. I was working the gate and Ida was doing the driving. I had shoved a heifer to the side and opened the gate for the cows to go through. One did not go through and ran back by me, kicking at me like a mule, with both hind legs at the same time. She missed and then saw Ida standing by the feed manger and headed right at her.

I shouted, "Jump through the manger!" but I think shock hit her and she stood still as a statue. I knew if the cow hit her head-on, Ida's head would hit the concrete part of the manger that was about 18 inches high. It could fracture her skull.

When the cow got within about two feet of her, Ida stepped aside and the cow passed her by but when she did she kicked again like a mule and caught Ida just under her hip. I'm not fibbing when I say she flew up into the air, before landing on her head on the dirty concrete. I ran to keep the cow away from her and then saw all the blood. She had a three-inch gash in her scalp on the side, just within the hair line. I helped her across a board fence into the house and wrapped a towel around her head.

We rushed to the emergency room at St. Mary's. I was afraid she was going to bleed to death before we arrived there. I watched as the doctor cleaned the sand and manure out of the wound and he had quite a job getting out the sand. It had worked up between her scalp and her skull. When he got it sewed up he asked if she was allergic to anything and she answered penicillin and tetanus antitoxin but could use tetracycline. About tetanus, it was a different problem as there was no alternative so he had us stay the rest of the day while he administered a small amount every 15 minutes watching her closely for a reaction and when he got the full amount injected we were allowed to go home, at about five o'clock.

Those were cheap days. For the medical work, we had to pay $191 but when we shipped the cow, along with another wild one, she hardly paid the bill. We had the whole Stockman gang up to help get those two cows on the truck. We had quite a time getting it done and used the unfinished axe and pick handles someone gave Ted. One thing about Francis and Fred Stockman along with J.B. DeWesplore, they had more guts than I ever did. We got those things loaded at midnight and hauled them to Columbia with the help of Fred and Francis. I spent the next day repairing fences and gates that got torn up. Another reason I wanted to get out of the cow business. About those handles Ted gave us, we busted every one up.

Ida says she remembers nothing of being kicked by the cow nor of climbing the board fence. She recalls when we left for the emergency room. I will always remember her flying up in the air and landing on her head and neck. It's a wonder she did not have a broken neck. I am thankful that she is, like all Stockmans, hard-headed. Otherwise she may not have been with me after that accident. Don't tell her that. Please.

Walking with Sadie

AFTER RECEIVING HIS PHD, Dave took a position with Iowa State and rented a home from a professor who had a sabbatical leave to Europe and we made a visit there. This was in 1975 and in the fall Dave purchased an older home. The old house did not have many electrical receptacles, so we rewired it so Carolyn could at least use a sweeper. We took Grandma along in the pickup for this visit. We left there on Thursday and headed for Ted's apartment in Brodhead, Wisconsin for a short visit before returning home.

While there, I did not feel well. At the time, I'd been feeling pressure in my chest. Dr. Gallagher said it was my heart and he used Everett and Mom as examples. I insisted he was wrong and many years later proved to be right. Anyway, after church we had dinner and I was sitting in the kitchen by the bar when I got an extremely odd feeling, like something was squeezing my chest, and the TV picture of a football game we were watching began to fade away. I thought I was having a heart attack. (I realize now I was having the same thing President Bush had while in Japan.)

They took me by ambulance to St. Clare's Hospital in Monroe and I spent the first week in intensive care and two more weeks in a room with one great guy, Mr. Ubert. The other roommate I had was not so great. He thought he had pneumonia and was continuously coughing up phlegm. He must have had many friends as he was getting many calls but he would not answer the phone. I knew the calls were not for me as I hardly knew anyone there but I still had to answer the phone and it burned me, especially this one call. When I said hello the man calling said, "Why you old son of a bitch, what are you doing in the hospital?" I could not think who would tell me that so I asked him who he was calling and of course he was calling for my roommate and there was a very embarrassed caller. I knew I was "something else" but I never dreamed of being a son of a bitch.

We had decided to carry our own insurance. The cost of the hospital stay was $5,545. The aftermath of this was taking much heart medicine (Nitro-Bid), thinking sometimes that the top of my head would blow off. The doctors said to wait two more weeks before going home and then do lots of walking.

This walking went well with beef cows and 300 acres of land when checking a pasture each day. Before, I checked the pastures but used the three-wheeler. Now I had to walk and took my faithful border collie Sadie along. The two of us became great friends, yet at times she made my Guardian Angel work extra hard. Sadie was nosy and one time ran up to smell a calf that had a bob-tailed Angus mother. Sadie promptly ran to me, as did the angry cow. I did a hell of a lot of jumping and yelling and got the old cow stopped about 10 feet away.

Another time when I was riding the Honda at night and Sadie took out after a cow, again the cow headed for me and just in time jumped right over the top of me and the three-wheeler. From then on, to save the Guardian Angel work, I tied Sadie and walked alone. We missed each other.

Hurt by a Calf

THE YEAR 1975 was full for us with those cows, grain to combine, and with more pasture than needed so that meant also combining orchard grass, fescue, and redtop seed. This was not as bad as we expected since those acres produced almost as well as wheat and oats. We also sold corn but not too much because our land was not as productive for that. When we first started farming, we went with soybeans which were great because you could sow them by just discing the soil. But we ended up feeding all the groundhogs and I can tell you those were hogs—some of 40-pound size could eat more stalks than a 1,000-pound cow! When the beans got about four inches high, it only took the groundhogs two days to clip off 10 acres. We blew up their dens, but that didn't help because the harder we worked the more they ate.

That year I had another bout in the hospital. Ida and I were vaccinating 400-pound calves for blackleg. Ted gave us a head gate to hold the calf's head while it was being treated. Rather than move the calves back and forth, we also installed another on the Kirchhoff farm. Here I was somewhat lazy and used the barn wall for one side of the chute. I paid for this mistake as the barn used upright siding which was nailed to a two-by-six middle plate as well as one on the top and the bottom for a 10-foot-high stable. The calves were stubborn (like people) and did not want to put their head in the chute. So big old me would get behind them and push them in.

We together had done this many times but on this occasion one of those calves spun around, placing his forefeet on that middle plate and pinning me against the outside part of the chute. His tail end went into my abdomen and he just slipped down and sat on me. By the time Ida got him off I was becoming sick and thought he may have burst my bladder. I sat for a while and finally had to urinate so I knew that had not taken place. We finished with the balance of the calves at about 11 o'clock and returned home.

I had a calf fence taken down and while Ida fixed dinner I carried the posts to a pile. I then needed to go to the toilet and when I did found a large lump and noted I had a rupture. After dinner we went to Dr. Gallagher and he confirmed it. He told us to have it repaired while it was a fresh tear so it would heal and hold better and not give way as many later repairs do. He called Dr. Shull and had me enter Memorial Hospital on Sunday morning to be ready for surgery on early Tuesday morning.

Monday was used to check my supposedly bad heart and also for a visit with the anesthetist. The only thing he checked was for loose teeth. That was a little beyond me yet I had no problems so I guess he knew his business. I was supposed to remain in the hospital for eight days but because I shunned pain medication, Dr. Shull asked me if I wanted to go home. If so, he would release me Saturday morning. If I did this it would be cheaper to come to his office to have the stitches removed on the next Tuesday. This suited me okay.

There was a special supplement in the Sunday News Tribune about this doctor. He was an extraordinary man and as a Marine doctor served his troops in field fighting in the South Pacific in World War II.

Break for Baptisms

WE TRAVELED SOUTH for two trips to visit Dave and family, who had moved from Iowa State to the University of Georgia at Athens. On our way back we toured the Southeast U.S.

We also went on a trip to baptize our new grandson, Paul. Thinking about this trip calls to mind when we also were in Ames, Iowa to baptize Christa and arrived just ahead of the worst blizzard of the century. Ted and Karen were to be her sponsors. Ted was not so lucky as us, as he chose U.S. 20 across northern Iowa and was held up because of the highway conditions. He stopped at a service station and parked his Olds facing the wind. Upon being told to go back to a motel they had passed, he found his car would not start. He had a block heater on it so he borrowed an extension cord to warm the motor but that did not help. He rode with a truck back to the motel and called us to say he was tied up. He called again later and told us to come after him and bring starting ether along with jumper cables. When the storm cleared we headed north to help him, passing trailer trucks that had blown over and lay in the ditch.

I was surprised to note that all the snow had blown from the fields and by each farmstead that stopped the wind we drove over a hump of snow that the highway department had packed down. One man had stopped by a farm home, where the family invited him and his 12-year-old son to stay. He left his son there, stating, "Since you have a dusk-to-dawn light that I can see, I will go back to stay with the car. If I feel unsafe, I can see the light and come to your home." Well the electric service went off so the man couldn't find the house and they found the man later frozen to death. This was only a short distance from where Ted was tied up.

When we got to Ted's car and opened the hood, we found the wind had packed snow around the motor so tight we had to clear it away to find the air cleaner. How the wind could blow the snow through the small spaces and the radiator is beyond belief. Surprisingly, with the ether it started right off and we headed back to Ames.

Accident with the Combine

TED MARRIED Barb Helland in 1977.

Ted and Barb's wedding

At about that same time, Karen married Andrew Gerke, Jr. and Bev graduated and took a position as purchasing agent for Montgomery Ward in Columbia.

And so we had an empty nest. Just Ida, me, and our dog Sadie.

Karen and Andrew's wedding

Because of hauling calves to market we built a loading pen on the two farms to make it easier for loading, and since the old Dodge was getting shaky like me, we traded for a used Chevrolet truck with 12,000 miles on it.

I had told you earlier that I would get back to the John Deere 45 combine and my scare. Here is the story.

My first two self-propelled combines each had a nine-foot cutter bar with a seven-foot wheel separation width and to keep it balanced with such a narrow wheel separation, we used water in the drive tires for weight to counteract the height. My 45 John Deere had a 10-foot cutter bar with a nine-foot six-inch wheel separation, meaning the tires extended to within three inches of the ends of the cutter bar. Since the width equaled the height the machine was not supposed to turn over and we did not have to fill the tires with water. Bull! In addition, with the wide wheels the cutter bar would not gouge the ground if a drive wheel hit a low spot as it did with the narrow width.

I will now tell you the importance of this. When combining beans with the two older ones you were putting about as much dirt in the grain hopper as soybeans. I recall one time when delivering a load of beans to the MFA Co-op, I was asked, "What in the hell are you using to combine these beans, a potato digger?" The dirt would pile in the center of the truck bed and the beans to the side and you had to get into the truck bed to shovel the dirt off as it would not slide when the truck was tilted up for unloading. The secret of this was that they did not degrade the beans so the dirt sold at the same price as the beans and was clear profit. That was unless you picked up a rock which played hell with the combine.

I was combining wheat on the home farm and at about quitting time I opened another terrace. This was below the last terrace, just above a creek that had timber growing along it. When I started a new terrace, I always straddled it to keep level as much as possible, especially if it was on steeper land. I combined across the field and turned across the end and down along the fence, then along the timber. I had not noticed, but a tree limb had got into the drive chain and threw it off, stopping up the return elevator. Since it was near quitting time I drove the combine home, cleaned out the elevator, and put the chain back on. I remember this was July 3. The next morning I gassed the combine up and headed to the field. This was about five acres and the last to combine on that farm.

I never thought I could afford a cab on a combine and in this case that kept me from being killed. Even being careful, accidents do happen and when you study those you wonder why. In going back to the field I crossed all the terraces head-on and on this last one that I had already straddled I put the thresher in gear and crossed the terrace on an angle going the backwards way around to put the grain unloading spout away from those trees and to complete the round of the night before. This put the full gasoline tank on the lower side and I guess that was a problem.

I slowed the combine down and watched just behind the cutter bar so I could stop if I saw a large rock before a wheel. While watching for a rock I saw the tire leave the ground and the thing went over so fast that I could not even jump off. When I hit the ground it knocked me out and when I came to I looked up and there it was standing over me. The only thing keeping it above me was the grain spout sticking in the ground. I looked over and saw the spout beginning to collapse and I crawled like heck to get from beneath it.

I stood and watched and when it gave way the darn combine rolled over on its top. I could picture it just continuing to roll down the hill. Through a new fence too. Was I surprised to see it stop with all wheels up in the air on just as much of a grade as when it left the ground. The only difference was that it was stopped on a five-foot square grain hopper and the operating platform. To be sure it smashed the heck out of both. A $15,000 outfit that looked real sad. Thank God I thought I could not afford a cab because, if I had one, I would have been trapped inside and it probably would have smashed me too.

I walked up to the house and told Ida what happened.

She asked, "Are you hurt?"

"I'm okay but my shoulder hurts like hell. Can you help me get the combine back on its wheels? We're gonna need two tractors."

"No way!" she said.

So I had to wait until my nephew-in-law got back from the 4th of July celebration that evening, and losing the time griped me.

We got the combine back on its wheels and he pulled it until it started and when it did there was so much smoke you couldn't see the field. I noted the damage of a twisted cutter bar, and a mashed platform, steering wheel, and seat. The grain bin looked like an accordion as did the return elevator. No insurance here either. I do believe in guardian angels and thanked God to still be alive. At least I was here to get it back in combining shape.

Be darn sure I had the tires filled with fluid which I now knew I should have done at the beginning and disregarded the bad advice I had been given. I headed from the tire shop to the John Deere dealer for parts. He told me to go to a machinery junkyard at Stover, Missouri that sold used parts. I took my nephew Jim Mertens along and upon us arriving there the owner unlocked the gate and said for us to see if he had one there. We had the big Dodge pickup and drove a circle through the largest amount of junk we ever saw. We were about to think he had none when at the end of the circle there sat an older and quite rusty one. We should have started that way to begin with.

I asked him what his asking price was and he said one-third the new cost. I could have jumped up and down with joy. Jim and I borrowed his tools and went to work getting the seat, steering wheel, platform, return elevator, and grain bin. That made a full load so we headed home.

The next day we went after the 10-foot cutter bar. The junkyard man took his high-lift and loaded it for us. The John Deere dealer's tip had helped a lot.

Jim and I put the platform on the combine and then the return elevator and this was an easy job. We started on the grain bin and ran into our real problem. It was smashed so bad we could not get to the bolts attaching it to the machine. We decided to drive a pointed crowbar through it and use our manure loader to stretch it partly back to the original position. We tried this and the darn thing would pick the complete combine from the ground and the bin would not give even half an inch. We had to use a cold chisel to cut enough metal away to get to the bolts.

Jim and I both forgot the elevator that carried the grain to the bin and had to drive all the way to Stover for the third time for a thing that did not weigh 100 pounds. Stupid! Well, kinda. Even so I was back in the combining business just over three days later and a hell of a lot wiser. Then too about a third of the wheat crop went to pay the parts expense. Cripes!

Well, for some reason we thought we needed a four-wheel-drive pickup. If you wonder why, I suppose it was that everyone else had one. We couldn't be different, could we? Then too, Bev wanted to buy our car and we would need another vehicle. So we now had two pickups. Both Dodge.

Selling the Farm

THERE MUST BE A REASON for a person to become crazy and I suppose it was our turn. Not only were we losing money on those beef cows, they were eating up the profits from the grain sales. When we were filing our tax returns the computer asked what had happened to the good investment returns, as in the three years we made only a little over $3,000 on our investment and these years cut into the Social Security we collect today. Well, retiring at 60 and not paying social security tax as a farmer didn't help either.

Our neighbor planted milo so close along the line fence that the cows reached through and ate the heads off. That fattened them up a little so they decided to reach after the second row and, as it was a dry year, 24 cedar posts snapped off and we had 40 cows along with their calves in the neighbor's milo field. To be sure, we had a hell of a job getting them back and never did get the calves out. We drove the cows to the barn lot and let them bawl for the calves so they came to their mothers. While they were coming, we were going back with steel fence posts that I drove in dry soil so hard I'd just as soon it had been concrete. The harder I drove, the madder I got and I told Ida, "This is it. Why in the hell are we working our asses off for nothing?" I said, "We are going to sell the farm and move to town."

This became a "we are—we are not—we are—we are not" thing between us, but I made up my mind if she did not want to move to town, I would myself. Getting older, I wanted to be near a grocery store and a doctor. I won our disagreement. She now agrees with me.

We sold our farm for $425 per acre for a total of $146,500, selling the house and one acre of land for $36,000 in cash (down payment) so we could use the money to purchase a home in California, Missouri. We did this so we could exchange the farm home for our home for income tax purposes. The buyer made a loan contract to cover our loan guaranteed with the Farmers Home Administration in excess of the loan for milk cows and needed equipment. At that time the going rate for interest with FmHA was 7%.

In checking with them we learned that we could carry the balance one point higher (8%) on a contract loan, with the government taking a second mortgage. We then carried a balance of $110,000. This way we could not lose our money. Five years down the road, this caused us a lot of grief. I will explain that later. We tried to find a good three-bedroom home but had to settle for a two-bedroom one and as we get older this does create less work for us. The contract sale helped as we only had to pay income tax on the monthly payments.

We decided to sell the beef cows and calves at sales barns rather than having a farm sale, so I recruited my friend John Wolken and we hauled two loads to Columbia on Tuesday and two loads to Olean on Friday. It took us two and a half months to do this. We lost somewhat because we had cows separated from their calves and so they could not be sold as pairs. Well! It really did not make much difference to me because I was just glad to get rid of them. Especially so when I recalled Ida and me putting square bales of hay into the barn the first year ourselves. Again beef cattle failed us as we cleared just over $24,000 for the herd. Thank God for having the cows long enough for capital gains for income tax.

Having smart kids, we again paid the price. Seems they were smart to move out of state so we could not beg for their help. Therefore we purchased our neighbor's small round baler for $300 and let the bales lie in the field, using electric fence to make the cows clean up the hay right in the pasture. As I said you never fail to learn a new way of being dumb. We had piles of waste hay lying in the field killing the next year's crop. Did a lot of harrowing to get that scattered about the next spring and while doing that I did some thinking. It was to trade our 45-foot hay bale elevator, small round baler, and new square baler with bale thrower for a large round baler and a bale carrier for the tractor with hydraulic cylinder to push the big bales into the big bale feeder. This worked but, by being placed outside, the bales became wet and froze. The cows would eat the inside and leave a ring that looked like great big road culverts. That meant I had to climb inside the feeders with an axe and chop the things apart and right now I do not mind calling them DAMN THINGS!

Retirement

Living in Town

WE PURCHASED OUR HOME "in the city" on January 7, 1978 just after my 60th birthday and I considered myself retired and Ida too. Well maybe. First she wanted to paint the purple and green rooms off-white and I do not blame her. (Who in the hell would paint a son's room purple even if he did want it?)

We moved to our home on January 27 and as far as I go, we were happy dwellers. Ida still thought of the country. As it turned out, I planted enough trees that she now thinks she is back in the country and says that if I die she is going to chop them down as darn if she is going to mow the grass around them. I remind her of the air conditioner effect from the trees and she replies, "Huh!" like I don't know what I am talking about. No comment from you either.

We got moved in after losing our alarm clock, table lamp, and we think now, a two-gallon crock jar that Ida used to make sauerkraut in. Somehow it disappeared and it was an antique too. I think we did move it and it got lost at a church picnic. I will be charitable in saying that I feel it was "copped."

So again my friend John Wolken and I went back to the farm to get the machinery ready for sale. We had the sale on the Kirchhoff farm because the family had already moved in although we retained possession of it until March 1. We again had a good sale by receiving over $44,000 for the machinery. When added all together we felt that we were now setting pretty for the balance of our lives. We even have to grant credit to President Carter for helping with the high interest of his day.

Replacing Rings

IDA NEVER WOULD REMOVE her small wedding rings that she said "were blessed with the vows of our marriage" and after 21 years they were completely worn out. I wanted her to have new rings and she insisted not. I think it was Beverly who helped me convince her that she would lose the stones and that they were "blessed" too. The engagement ring had one diamond and the wedding band three and one had already been lost. It was replaced along with the others in a new pair as closely matched as possible.

Be assured the old ones were saved and today they are in a beautiful picture frame with a Christmas tree covered with all old beads, those rings, 4-H award medals, old wristwatches, earrings, and every old thing that had been saved throughout the years. The only thing missing is my old wedding band that was lost somewhere in our home as I had quit wearing it because it had worn so thin that it began to cut my finger. It too was replaced, but kept for Sunday wear. I now wear my band steady and Ida saves hers for going places so others can see what she now has is fancy.

You really need to see this picture and if you do come around we will show it to you. Our daughter Beverly made the thing for her mother. The base of the tree has an open locket I had given Ida 48 years ago with both of our pictures. There too is the beaded bracelet with the name Mertens that was placed on David's wrist when he was born. All the others had just a paper band.

Picture frame with mementos

Seeing the Country

IN 1979 David was set to travel about the States to speak at seminars and he offered to pay all the expenses if we would come with him and use our trailer. He would finance it with his flying expense and motel money.

The first such trip was to Tucson, Arizona at the university there. We and his family lived in the trailer and saw much country while there.

While David was speaking, we toured the community. The best was a Catholic church that was built by the Spanish in the early 1600s and has the most beautiful interior paintings I have ever seen. It sits in the country and is still in use by a Native American tribe as it was when it was built. Another place we toured was the Davis-Monthan Air Force Base where I admired the old planes of my day that helped win the war. We also went to Douglas and across the border into Mexico.

From there we headed for San Diego, crossing over the desert sand on the interstate that was built over a roadway which at one time was a plank road. Believe this, they just pushed some of the plank road sections alongside of the interstate so people could see the remains of the old road. We also crossed East Diablo Canyon and here the highway can scare the hell out of you. It is also the place where Father Junipero Serra crossed with 300 head of cattle for the California Missions using 30 vaqueros. That seems almost impossible but they did. You need to visit this canyon.

We were driving a 1978 Dodge customized van, which we'd bought in 1979 at a great discount. It had a 360-cubic-inch motor and handled the trailer very well, yet I doubted if we would get out of the canyon.

What scared me was the many water barrels along the way that could be used to add water, as it must have meant cars often overheated in that canyon. We cut off the air conditioner so as not to put any extra stress on the system. Must have worked, since we did eventually get out of that canyon. Dave wanted the van, so today it sits in Belleville, Wisconsin. It now has over 100,000 miles on it but makes an occasional trip to Missouri.

I would love to tell you about all our travels but I don't want to drag my story along. But I will tell you this. In the next 16 years we traveled about and saw practically all the contiguous United States, as well as Mexico and Canada. Hawaii too. Take our advice and don't sit at home. Go see our country and make memories. And don't wait as long as we did.

On our travels we used the slide-in camper twice to the southeast and south then traded it for a 22-foot travel trailer. We used that for 27,000 miles and then bought a motor home. We put 42,000 miles on that but were never satisfied as you could not hold your camping space. With a trailer you can unhook and let it hold your space and travel about with your car. So the motor home was traded for another trailer and we used it to travel west. Ida began to worry that something might happen to me on a trip and she would have to get the trailer back and refused to. So in 1990 we made our last trip and me at the great age of 73.

Serving the Community

IDA DID MANY THINGS to benefit others and I'd like to brag on her a little here. She was the first to become election judge and clerk and did such a good job that it left me out. Time and time again she was called and responded. She served as 4-H leader for many years and has a great certificate to show for her effort. She also served on the University of Missouri Extension Council for two terms and stood her ground against unwise decisions. She told me this so I know it is true.

She and I became Honorary State Farmers because of our work with the Future Farmers of America, California Chapter because Ida did all of this work for this award and I will agree with that.

Ida was called to be a juror in Federal District Court in Kansas City and had quite a chore getting out of it. She declined because she gets migraine headaches. She had to furnish the court her prescription for her migraine medicine. They released her and I think she offered a prayer many nights in thanksgiving.

Just after Ida's dad died, Mom came home with us to spend some time "away from memories." While she was with us, I advised her to appoint a Markway as administrator of the estate. I told her that since she was a Markway, they would look after her interest. She thought that to be a good idea as I had also explained that settling an estate created divisions within a family. Her son Willard told Mom, while Dad was still alive, that it should be family as it was no one else's business. He suggested Mom, Ida, and himself as administrators and she followed his suggestion. As it turned out, Mom knew nothing and Willard, with a drinking problem, was not much help and so the chore fell on Ida's shoulders. One result was an angry brother who thought Dad had promised him the estate. It was settled, but with Ida's brother David feeling sorry for himself and shying away from the family about the settlement 22 years ago. Never appoint a close family member to administer an estate if you do not want trouble.

Ida

As for me, throughout the years I did my service too. I was Chairman of the Farm Bureau Dairy Council, doing promotion and research on dairy product sales, serving two three-year terms. I was Chairman of Jefferson City Dairy Council for four years, working with schools to improve usage of milk and promote the benefits of milk to growing children. I was Chairman of District #18 Mid-America Cooperative for two three-year terms. Also, I was a member of the resolutions committee of St. Louis Division of Mid-America Dairymen Inc. for two terms. I was a board member of the California, Missouri MFA Bulk Oil Company Plant for eight years, during which I attended conventions and toured refineries.

I served on the Rural Fire Protection District at the time the district purchased a four-wheel-drive water support truck. We had learned from many farm fires that the extra water had to come from isolated farm ponds.

I was elected to the Moniteau County Agricultural Improvement Association and served until the association was disincorporated. I helped sell the equipment to a used mining replacement company in Kansas City and paid off the mortgage and distributed the balance to the membership. This was after I worked for the association hauling lime.

I was a delegate of the locally owned MFA Cooperative Association to three conventions of the home MFA State Parent Association. This cooperative was formed in 1917 by a group of people including S.E. Lawson and Mr. William Bower, my nephew Quentin's wife's uncle. The association did over three million dollars of business per year (in the 1970s). Due to complaints about noise from grain drying and grinding it was moved outside of the city limits. It was decided to borrow money from the Bank of Cooperatives to make the move. Tipton, Missouri also had a locally owned co-op that was in a financial bind. To make the loan, the bank asked our co-op to take over the Tipton branch loan and combine the two co-ops. This was a mistake because assuming the debt load of a poor business along with the building expense, our co-op could not overcome the debt load and as a consequence both were assumed by the state MFA. I think now that this was planned so they could take over the locally owned co-ops. This caused Ida and me to lose the $4,200 equity we had in our association. We did get to deduct this loss from our income tax.

I was called and served on the jury in a felony case. This was a sad affair as two young men robbed and almost beat to death an elderly man along Highway 50 just west of McGirk, Missouri. They had heard that the old bachelor had money hidden in his home. At that time both were only 18 years old. The old fellow tried to tell them he had no money and they beat him to try to make him talk. One of these was a Wheat who lived just west of Emil and Cath and was known as a troublemaker. The other was from Fulton, Missouri. Their lawyer was a Callaway County legislator by the name of Holt. He was crippled like my mother and was somewhat of a scamp himself. He kept getting continuances for six years before the case came to trial. He had his reason; he knew the old man was losing his eyesight.

I thought this trial was certainly an injustice to the old man. While these boys stole only $10, they had made it a felony by beating him. When choosing the jury, Mr. Holt asked my name and I told him Mertens. He asked, "Any kin to the Mertens who run the construction company in Fulton?" and I said, "They are my nephews." He said, "I'll take you."

Since the old man was blind, he could no longer identify either of the criminals and the only other witness was the sheriff. Mr. Holt (in my opinion) was not aboveboard. When they questioned the jury, the judge told the sheriff to remove all witnesses and guard the door. The sheriff did this by standing in the courtroom side of the door. After the old fellow could not identify either of the men the sheriff was called as the next witness. Since the sheriff heard the jury being chosen, Mr. Holt challenged him as a witness and he could not testify. Of course Mr. Holt thought he had won the case but by that time he had a very angry judge. The judge refused to dismiss the case and he gave both the attorney and the sheriff a good going-over in words.

We sat in the jury box for two hours while they argued and finally Mr. Holt plea-bargained the case to a misdemeanor and had both men plead guilty. These men were now 24 years old and one had married and had his wife and two-year-old daughter with him. The judge told both that they deserved more sentence than he could give them. He said, "You pleaded guilty so I am going to give you the maximum sentence and that is six months in jail and a fine of $180 each." We were dismissed, knowing these two did not come out ahead by taking the old man's $10.

I might add this. Mr. Leonard Kirchhoff of McGirk was also a juror and on our way home we stopped at Reed's Service Station for a Coke and Mr. Kirchhoff said, "You know, I could look at that one SOB and see that he was guilty." The one he referred to was the most insolent I ever saw. He had his shirt unbuttoned down to his belly button and stood before the judge with the attitude of "I couldn't care less." Both of us jurymen had said that nothing would stand in the way of our being fair. In this case he made that quite a chore.

The people of eastern Moniteau County voted for forming the Public Water District #2. I'm sure this was because Groner-Pickard Engineering of Jefferson City did a lot of legwork, knowing they would get the job. It was also pushed by the Farmers Home Administration. After the vote, the circuit court of our district, of which Moniteau County was a part, appointed a five-member board. They were Wesley Baine: Chairman, Clement Mertens: Vice-chairman, Richard Call, Dwayne Bolin, and Curtis Kirchner: members. It became our job to get easements for the right-of-way for free. This meant a lot of driving, mostly in the evening and for free also. It did not take long for us to realize we had a headache type job.

We had to get these easement rights for 36 miles of line. We chose Groner-Pickard to be our engineers and John Kibbe as our attorney. We received a $198,000 grant from the government (you taxpayers) and borrowed another $212,000. With all the work, we had only about six who would not give the right-of-way and two of them were along Highway 50 and we could bypass them by using highway right-of-way. The other four were land owners who had FmHA loans and it didn't take the FmHA supervisor long to get those easements for us. I will admit that while we were dairymen, we wanted this water because we then would have no worries about the water quality passing St. Louis inspection. The sad part was that since we were on the end of the line it did not arrive before we were out of the dairy business.

I served on this board until we moved into the city of California and turned my position over to Everett's son-in-law, Raymond "Estel" Bishop.

Then too after moving to the city I was elected a member of the FmHA County Committee Loan Review Board and served one three-year term, ending in the third year as chairperson. Since California is a town of less than 10,000, all housing loans made by the U.S. government go through the county office. Here I learned how people took advantage of the government. I fought the first Public Rental

Housing loan because it only took renters away from apartment owners here in California and I knew of two who were widows. In the case I speak of, they loaned the money to one landowner and two lawyers from Eldon by the name of Fountain. These are the three large apartment buildings just west of California. Much of the money was a grant and did not have to be paid back. Even worse they are paid $255 per month for each apartment by the taxpayers even if the apartments are not rented. Then too, two-thirds of the rental money does not stay in California but goes to Eldon.

This past year another group of homes were built through the same landowner but this time by two financiers from Marshall, Missouri. They even brought in their own building crew and lumber from Marshall and again this money is leaving town.

Be assured these plans do not benefit the poor as much as these rich people from out of town. Also food stamps are of much concern to farmers as well as grocery store owners and they will fight to keep these programs, even more so than the recipients. I note that both of these programs are targeted for an increase at the same time others are to pay for the supposed deficit reduction.

Volunteering at Church

IDA WAS FIRST TO BE ELECTED to the parish council at our church and served for one term of three years. She was elected as Chairman of the Church Quilters for two terms. Each year those ladies return $800 to $1,200 for church support. This began in the old school basement and has lasted for over 15 years. She has also helped for many years with the ladies who furnish dinners for the mourners after parish funerals. And she's served two terms of four years each as Chairwoman.

She also made the baptism garments for many parish babies. This was after the change in the ritual of baptism. At that time our pastor was Father Missey and he chose a sort of bib to place over the baby and afterward this was presented to the parents. Ida, as the embroiderer, hand-stitched a candle with flame and a cross with a ripple of the water of baptism. She made dozens of these bibs. When Father Daly became our pastor, he just wanted a plain satin sheet with a fringe on each end and she made many of those. Then when Father Gillgannon became pastor, he went back to the bib style and she is now making those.

Baptism bib and sheet with fringe [9]

Ida also made the large Resurrection Banner that was used for many years throughout Easter time as well as the other banners for the changes of church season. When we got Sister Anna Boessen (from St. Thomas), she decided they were no longer good enough and purchased new ones through the Sisters' Home. These did not come cheap. I do not need to tell you that got Ida's ire. Sister Anna is our pastoral minister.

For me, my church work began with the Student Union at Sacred Heart Parish in Columbia and in the fundraising I have already told you about. Here in California I also served as treasurer for the school bus even after we turned the operation over to the church as I mentioned.

Ida and me in our parish photo

After Vatican II we found a lot of resentment toward change so we just never could get people to shake hands for the sign of peace. It was hard for me to accept these changes also because it was so far away from the church we were brought up in. While Father Missey was our pastor he really did not accept the changes either. When he left the parish we got Father Keating as our pastor and at that time I was elected as a member of the building committee for a new church. Father Missey began to put pressure on the members to become leaders for the change and started with trying to get some to become lectors. He kept after Paul Imhoff and me to be the first. I agreed and this helped me as I learned to stand before people, which you will hear more about later.

I brought the missal home and studied and did the first one. I asked Father Keating how I did and he said okay only you need to slow down. Ida was not so charitable. She said I sounded like an old phonograph record played at high speed. I did learn to slow down.

I served seven years on the parish council and was serving when our school burned and we had a big fight on our hands to get a $17,000 increase on insurance. I could tell quite a story about this but for the good of the church I had better not.

I was chosen as Charter Grand Knight of the Annunciation Council #9271 and given the job of getting the council going in California. We hosted the sale of the old church equipment in our first year as a council. Today I would not be so fast in accepting this kind of chore but Father Daly insisted. I served two terms. Here I want to thank Rick Kolb for all the help I received from Helias Council in Jefferson City and their First Degree Team. Rick was Grand Knight there at that time.

Ida and I together were chosen by Father Greene to be Extraordinary Ministers of the Holy Eucharist along with eight others. We, at that time, had to be approved by the bishop and had a commissioning on a Sunday afternoon. We each were given a large candle and marched through the church in the ceremony. We, like the priest, had to wash our hands before and after. There was a plate of water for our use. It sat on the altar. Quite a change today since now you only have to volunteer with no ritual whatever.

Our new church was not built to be very usable for ushering, especially during Communion. It is built in the shape of a diamond and the people were really confused so it was decided that the people could better do this themselves. From the time of that decision, they began to call ushers "greeters" and their duty was to open the door for people to enter and welcome them at the same time. Also they passed the collection baskets and after Mass handed out the bulletins to the people as they left. We had such a thing as offertory bearers and after collection it became their duty to take the offering to the priest at the table (used to be the altar). If for some reason these people were absent it also became the duty of the greeters. So it came about that Ida and I did each of these chores on our assigned Sunday.

We both served two terms on the Ministry Commission and also two terms on the church picnic committee as chairpersons. Quite a job. Then too Ida, along with five others, leads in saying the rosary before the eight o'clock Mass each Sunday. We, along with Gertrude Swillum, served as money counters for several years taking our month of that duty when it was our turn.

Aiding the Extension Service

As you know, I, along with Ida, took great part in the Extension Service. The University of Missouri as well as Lincoln University in Jefferson City were land grant colleges. This act was passed during the civil war by President Lincoln. They were given public land that they could sell, and used that money for farm product experiments to better the country as they increased production and yields.

To get information about this greatly increased production to the people, the Extension Service was formed. I can't tell you exactly when, but I feel it to be either the year of 1912 or 1920. The government paid the college professors' wages and put at least one in each county throughout the country. Some counties had more. They were called extension agents but farmers called them county agents.

These agents did pass on some mistakes to the farmers but the good ideas were more abundant. We have to admit that we benefited and I am proud to say our eldest son is an agricultural research scientist with the Department of Agriculture. He travels widely in England, France, New Zealand, Australia, and Brazil (these are the ones I can think of). Our second son is a doctor of veterinary medicine. Both have remained with agriculture.

The only expense to the counties for the Extension Service was office space, equipment, furniture, and a secretary. This was in the 1970s and the costs and wages were much below those of today. Here I might add that today we have priced many items off of the market for lower income people, yet we call this progress. The gain from this goes to the government because they collect more income tax.

Extension center award

So it came about that many county courts (now called commissioners) declined to fund these offices to save money and one such county was Osage County.

Since we were using these offices widely, they called upon me to make a presentation to the Osage County Court and people at a banquet served in the Lion's Hall in Westphalia, Missouri. The meeting began with a prayer by Father Edwin Schmidt. It was opened by the chairperson of the Osage Extension Council and she spoke of the advantages of the "greening" of Osage County with improved pastures since Osage County is primarily a beef cattle county; because it is also a timber county. This person was a Mrs. Zitka. A veterinary professor from the School of Veterinary Medicine was to speak after me.

I wrote and gave this presentation:

Ladies and gentlemen, I stand before you tonight quite shaky as it is my first before a group of people. I do want you to understand that the unusual noise from up here is my knees a-knocking and not rocks rattling in my head.

Before I begin, I want to tell you this story. A young Jaycee was called upon by a festival committee to provide three speakers and each would be allowed 15 minutes. The young man called upon the superintendent of schools to speak on education, the town banker on economics, and the town doctor on sex and morality.

He introduced the superintendent, saying he will talk on education. The superintendent began, saying, "Ladies and gentlemen, it gives me great pleasure …", and continued on and on for 20 minutes. The banker started the same way and talked almost as long as the superintendent. By this time the young fellow began to get nervous and whispered to the doctor, "We are running out of time, can you cut your speech short?" The doctor answered, "I think I can."

The young man then introduced the doctor, saying he will speak on sex. The doctor approached the podium and began his speech saying, "Ladies and gentlemen, it gives me much pleasure" and then he sat down.

Tonight I hope I am not so long-winded as to be boring like the superintendent and banker; yet like the doctor have enough to say to get my point across.

Each of us can call to mind a farmer who, having decided he could no longer make a living as a farmer, decided to quit farming and move to the city. When he left his community, he no longer returned anything to the area economy and many times became a problem for the city. I want to tell you a story just the opposite of this. I have a friend who realized that he had advanced as far as he could expect to go and decided to quit his job and become a farmer. He and his wife purchased a little run-down and eroded 80-acre farm and set out to become farmers. They had just enough savings to make the down payment and when they moved into their new area I am sure their new neighbors considered them to be a joke.

He knew he needed help so he was not ashamed to approach his prosperous neighbor and ask for his advice. He approached the Extension Service and spoke with the agricultural engineer about terracing the farm and building an approved pond. He went to the agronomy specialist and as he terraced, he planted his pasture and determined his most productive fields. He joined DHIA (Dairy Herd Improvement Association) and saw his herd milk production go from just under 9,000 pounds to over 17,000. He added to his farm through many years and on each farm terraced, limed, and phosphated the land to soil test. He and his family cleared many fence rows and combined many small fields into larger ones. He saw his 80 acres grow into 340 and become productive ones. The family built many miles of fences.

His most important achievement came about when he and nine other farmers were recruited to join the University of Missouri Computer Farm Record Keeping in 1964. It was then he learned what farming was all about. In 1970 the family won the Greater Chamber of Commerce of Kansas City, Missouri Farm Management Award. Just two months ago he was offered $190,000 for his dairy operation and he turned the offer down.

Before I came in front of you tonight, I did some research work in Moniteau County. In 1954 the county judges expended $.50 per farm family toward Extension. My friend paid just $34 in taxes and returned $5,400 to the area economy. Last year the judges expended $3.50 per family and my friend paid $960 in taxes and returned over $44,600 to the area economy.

To me that means six better-than-$7,000 jobs in our county. It means that six families will remain in Moniteau County and return their earnings to the economy.

Mrs. Zitka just told you about the "greening" of Osage County. Get into your car on a Sunday afternoon and when you note one of the farms with improved pastures, stop and talk with the people and you will learn that every one of them was willing to continue his education in farming.

Ladies and gentlemen, I see no better way to do this than through the Extension Service. Thank you.

I was surprised at the response I received. Many shook my hand, yet the greatest compliment I received was when my old agricultural engineer friend, Hubert Krautmann, shook my hand and said, "I didn't know you could bullshit like that."

The veterinary professor in making his speech said, "I came down here with many great ideas to impart to you. I find that Mrs. Zitka and Mr. Mertens said it all."

Needless to say, the county judges continued funding the Osage County Office and still do today. I got myself another job like this one and it was to speak before all 114 county-elected Extension Council members in the University of Missouri Field House. I will get to that in the final chapter.

Guardian Angels

TODAY AS I BEGIN THIS CHAPTER the date is August 23, 1993. Yesterday Ida and I attended the 50th wedding anniversary celebration of my old school mate Archie Siebeneck and his wife Helen. To my surprise I got to see only a few schoolmates as the others are now dead, yet Archie and I are still here. I had one especially in mind and that was Walter Lauf, and since he is Archie's brother-in-law I was sure he would be there. Upon asking I was told that he is not doing well and was too sick to come. At our age that will soon be the same for us as we are "looking at the end of time."

Yet I met an 86-year-old man with a mind as sharp as a tack. He was Roy Henley and my former school teacher. This man walked up to me and said, "You are Clement Mertens," and he said, "I taught you in third grade." After talking with him, I had to know he was right as he told me so many things, like my nickname "Buben." Think about how a man can remember and recognize a pupil nine years of age some 66 years later. He asked, "How are Emil, Felix, and Everett?" and I had to tell him, "They are no longer with us." He told me that year was the last he taught school as he had married and he said, "I had to quit teaching because I could not support a wife on $30 a month." What a wonderful afternoon spent remembering the old days.

The day before, we had attended the wedding of Don Stockman's daughter and while there learned that my cousin Ben Mertens had gotten run over by a hay baler on the heavy wheel side. Since we were near his home, we went to visit with him that afternoon. He is 80 and I wonder why he is still messing with a hay baler. He told me how lucky he was that, because of a young kid he had working for him, he did not get killed.

The baler had begun giving them trouble so he stopped the tractor and stopped its motor, leaving the power takeoff in gear. He was positive he had the tractor out of gear. He worked on the baler and was going to test it and told the boy to start the tractor motor saying, "It is out of gear so all you have to do is turn the ignition key and it should start and the shaft will run." He was standing just ahead of the heavy wheel and it ran across his left leg and along the inside of his right leg, pulling the muscle away from the bone. He yelled when it started up toward his body and the boy got it stopped just in time.

Sunday he told us he was healing real well only he had fluid in the muscle on his right leg and the fluid is slow in leaving. He spent two days in the hospital then was told to go home and use a walker and now had graduated to a cane. These things do happen as we just do not think. A good example of what one should not do, yet each of us knows we did these kinds of things ourselves many times and, as Ben said, were lucky. Maybe it was our guardian angel of olden times.

So I now will tell all of you to be careful in what you do.

Health Issues

I TOLD YOU about the "bad heart" I had, according to the diagnosis from Dr. Gallagher, and the heart medicine I was taking. And I had told you I disagreed with this. One night I got so tight in my chest that I thought I was going to choke. Ida called Dr. Gallagher and he said to get to emergency and have them call Dr. Jack Sanders. When we arrived they put me in intensive care and told me that Dr. Sanders would see me the next morning. When he arrived he told me I was not sick enough to be in intensive care and that they needed the room for someone sicker than I was. They put the monitor by the nurses' station and he said he would see me the next morning. For some reason, a Sister put an oxygen tube in my nose only a short time before he came to see me.

"What you got that thing on for?" he asked.

I told him, "I don't know."

He said, "You don't need that" and took it off.

What he said next made me lose all respect that I may have had for him because he said it right before my roommate.

My roommate, a Mr. White from Holts Summit, commented, "He sure thinks he is a smart SOB, don't he?"

Dr. Sanders told me there was nothing wrong with my heart and when I got it off my mind I would be a lot better off. He let me think it was all in my head.

"Tell my doctor that," I said.

He replied, "Throw your heart medicine away."

I told him I wanted a stress test.

He took me by taxi to Memorial Hospital and while walking on the treadmill my bad knee began to hurt and I started limping. He then stopped the machine and asked why I was limping and I told him I did not know I was but that I did have a bad knee. He told the nurse to give me a nitro pill for under my tongue and after I rested to send me back to St. Mary's. Rose came to see me that evening and told me that the heart monitor looked great. I asked her why he gave me the nitro pill and she said they always do, just in case.

The next morning Dr. Bregnent discharged me. He was somewhat more diplomatic than Dr. Sanders. He took me into another room and said that if you were ever told you had a heart problem, then each time you got a strange feeling you would think it was your heart. He said to tell yourself, "It's not my heart" and that it would take about two years before you really convinced yourself. He also told me to get off the rigid diet I was on. "You have a heavy-boned body so don't try for 170 pounds." He said my frame could handle 210 pounds easily and I was already down to 204. He then discharged me. I think Dr. Bregnent is an internist and I know that Dr. Sanders is a noted cardiologist. Neither one told me, although they evidently were right about my heart, what the problem might be. They just referred me back to Dr. Gallagher. I fault both doctors here as I was back to where I started.

Here my DVM son came to the rescue. He said, "Dad, make them send you to a gastroenterologist since you always thought it to be a digestive problem."

I kept telling myself every time I had a tight feeling that it was not my heart but that did not make the feeling go away. One Friday night I got so much pressure I became scared but toughed it out. Ida called Dr. Gallagher for an appointment on Monday and I told him to send me to a gastroenterologist and he said, "What for?" and I answered, "To find out what the hell is wrong with me."

He said, "I already know."

I said, "Do you really want to know what Dr. Sanders said?" and he said yes. I told him he said to throw my heart medicine away and I would be better off.

He said, "I know better."

What does one do in a case like this? I insisted on being sent to the hospital and he made the arrangements. I told him not to send me back to Dr. Sanders and he asked why and I told him that I thought he was a smart aleck.

He answered, "He is quite snippy, isn't he?"

When I got to St. Mary's I was checked right to the fourth floor with heart patients and I was angry. The next morning, after having a bad night with one of the spells, I called in the nurse and asked her to feel how tight I was. My abdomen was like a rock. I told her to make a report of this and tell the doctor. She told me to get up and walk and that I may be able to work it off. To walk around the nurse's station where they could watch me.

The next morning Dr. Boyer came to see me and said, "You are my patient." He sat on the bed beside me and I asked him why he was here after I had asked for a gastroenterologist. He explained that he was an internist.

After our talk he said, "I am inclined to agree with you. I think your doctor is wrong. But don't be too hard on him because if you fell dead right here beside me I could not say whether you died from a heart attack or acute indigestion without having an autopsy performed since the two are so closely interrelated."

I liked Dr. Boyer because he did not act like I was nutty as Dr. Sanders did.

Dr. Boyer sent me through a lower GI test. The radiologist was an elderly man about six and a half feet tall. As the technician was moving the X-ray machine over my body, the radiologist was watching the monitor. "Stop!" he told the technician. Then, "See that spot?"

She continued over my lower body and upon going back he had her stop again to study what he saw. Here I was proven right but not in the manner I wanted.

"You have a mass on your ascending colon," he said, "but I think it is a spasm. I want you to come back for another GI in 90 days and if that mass is still there we will have to open you up to note what it is."

Of course, 90 days put me into another $506 deductible period on my insurance, where had he said 60 days, I would have still been covered.

This waiting really got to me, as no one wants to feel like they are bursting.

One day I noted in the California newspaper where the Veterans Service Officer was going to be in the city and I told Ida, "I'm going to find out why I cannot get into a VA Hospital."

In the Army we'd heard so many promises of how well we were going to be taken care of as veterans. It gripes me because of all the crap we had to take while training and I was only paid the great amount of $21 per month, but it was supposed to be worth it because of the promise of medical care for the rest of my life. Right now I'm denied veteran hospital benefits because Ida and I have too much money to pass a means test. I should not complain because those old World War I vets were only paid $13 per month. Yet the few that are left can get hospital benefits. What really gets me is that if you are a dope user or a drunk you can be admitted because it is thought to be from the stress of war and thus connected to your service. Well it's like the old saying goes "all is (not) fair in love and war" and the many "Dear John" letters during the war proved that. Oh, well.

The officer was just sitting there with no customers and asked, "What can I do for you?"

I was angry and asked, "Why can't I get into a VA Hospital? My doctor told me he never could get a patient in. He couldn't even get himself into one when he got emphysema." In my case he would no longer try.

I explained my health issues to the officer and he said, "You will be in the hospital within seven days if you can answer this question: If you had to have open heart surgery could you afford it?"

"Probably, but I doubt there would be much left."

He answered, "That is all I want to know. You will receive a letter within seven days," and I did, although I was supposed to wait those 90 days.

When you think about it, there are some times when you have too much faith in your doctor. Here we had a man that we respected because he had treated us so nice that we never felt he could be wrong. Maybe after reading you will learn that if you have any doubt, get another doctor and not one your doctor refers you to.

I had to go through many tests and they probably saved my life. I learned that my issues included a spastic colon, irritable bowel syndrome, and that I could not digest milk (after all those years as a dairyman!) because I had a lactose problem due to fermentation in my small intestines that would cause irritation that would trigger the colon spasms. I also learned that I had a cholinergic problem. As this was explained to me, one's body has both voluntary and involuntary systems. Involuntary is an action that you have no control over, such as your heartbeat or your digestive tract. Your body automatically sends these messages to your brain and the brain sends a message correcting the problem. In digestion, your stomach sends messages to your brain. An example: If you ate a lot of fat, this is slow to digest so your stomach sends a message to your brain telling it to send a great amount of bile from your liver to aid digestion and to hold the food in your stomach so it can complete its job.

When you are cholinergic (this generally is physiological), if you are under stress, it will cause your brain to send a wrong message back to your stomach. Like, if you need bile, your brain sends a message back telling your stomach to dump into your small intestines and if it does you are in trouble. I was told there's a drug to correct this but it's a mind-altering drug and they advised using it only as a last resort. So I was placed on three teaspoons of Metamucil three times a day to keep something soft in my colon as they learned that by keeping something mushy there the colon would not go into a blocking spasm. The doctor told me that a colon could go into such a tight spasm as to block blood flow and become gangrenous and then I recalled that Ida's sister-in-law Shirley Stockman's dad died from that within three days.

While in the VA Hospital I had a tumor removed from my forehead and that saved me from another serious problem. After I got out of surgery, I was told that they were sending me back to Medicine.

"Why?" I asked.

The doctor said, "You will find out about that there."

So they took me back and there I was told that when taking the blood sample for surgery they found I had 82% degeneration of my liver. The first thing they asked was whether I used dope and that made me angry and I told the doctor he knew better than that. He then laughed and asked if I had ever worked in a chemical factory and I told him as a tire man I used much benzene and as a farmer much pesticides.

He said, "I am going to put you into the computer to find if any other VA Hospital had any such problems," and then told me to come back in a week. When I did, I was told they found my problem and it was the drug hydrochlorothiazide (a diuretic) that Dr. Gallagher had me taking for high blood pressure. I am allergic to that drug and now carry a card saying that no one should give me a prescription for it. It took about a year for my liver to get back from 48 to 54. The surprising thing is that I did not even know about the liver issue. There is a warning now on this drug of this serious side effect.

I really thought lots of that group of doctors and can say I was never treated better in a hospital. They were tops. I had my first colonoscopy and a polyp removed. I still have my card but was sad when told I had to meet a means test from then on. I haven't been back since.

To think of all those years taking those drugs that were wrong. I told Ida that I was not going back to Dr. Gallagher because I thought that a doctor should at least listen to what your symptoms were. Dr. Gallagher became hard-headed. I don't think he could admit he was wrong.

We discussed this with Ida's niece, Dr. Rebecca Lueckenhoff, and she suggested Dr. Domke whom she worked with as a resident at the Medical Center and the VA Hospital. This was back in 1985 and so far we both are well satisfied. Anyway we are both still here.

Legal Woes

I SAID EARLIER that I would tell you about the problems we ran into after taking out that $110,000 mortgage when we sold the farm. My cholinergic stress came about because the husband and wife team we loaned the $110,000 to, Mr. and Mrs. Pettit, got into one hell of a squabble over the man falling in love with his neighbor's wife. This led to a nasty divorce with him giving her a property they owned at Jamestown for $20,000 and a third mortgage for another $20,000 with a blanket lien on everything. She caught him selling mortgaged property and she took him into a trustee's sale. To head her off, he filed bankruptcy and that tied all of us up.

It took eight months for us to get our money and we had to sue the bankruptcy trustee, who was a Columbia lawyer, to get it. This was because we had a secured loan of the farm and, as Mr. Pettit and his attorney Rudolph "Rudy" Veit listed the farm at $140,000, the trustee thought he should hold the farm for sale at that amount and thereby pay the unsecured creditors. It was here where we and Mrs. Pettit's attorney ran into a little problem with Rudy. I never had an idea how unfair a bankruptcy court could be until this hearing.

Mrs. Pettit's attorney knew that her husband had titled more than $40,000 of trucks, tractors, and a pickup just before filing bankruptcy, saying he did so to his mother who had loaned him money. Her attorney had him over the barrel as he still had to file joint income tax with his wife and she, with those papers, could prove him filing a fraudulent petition.

Rudy jumped up and objected that we were not having an income tax hearing and the darn bankruptcy judge sustained him, leaving him walking away with over $74,000, part of which was the MFA Co-op Association loan for over $45,000, causing it to go broke too. Those losing were St. Mary's Hospital of $5,000, our young veterinary with over $4,000, a baby doctor in Jefferson City with a delivery of a baby with $1,200, and Russellville Exchange with over $23,000. To help someone beat another through bankruptcy only puts them in a position where they too have to file a petition.

Beverly had taken a law course and I had her big old law book here and reading it helped me get back at them. Through FmHA I got a copy of the petition they had filed and saw many fraudulent items. This time we were not at a hearing so I called Rudy and got a receptionist and she told me if I were a creditor that he would not talk with me. I told her he had better, and if I did not receive a call from him by five o'clock, he would hear from me. She again assured me he would not talk with me.

I then wrote Rudy a letter and pointed out every mistake (as he later admitted) that he had made as I had furnished Mr. Pettit with a computer printout and could prove the items. I also told him if I did not hear from him within 10 days I was going to have the U.S. Marshall of the Kansas City District pick up both him and Mr. Pettit for fraud. You can bet I heard from Rudy in two days telling me that, after reading my letter, he really did not think Mr. Pettit realized what I had.

What was odd about this was that Mr. Pettit was to remain on the farm and guarantee everything to be there and had skipped out and no one knew where he had gone. Rudy had him here in another two days and promptly released us of all claims. We received over $88,000 plus interest and all attorney fees other than the $274 I had paid in advance.

Rudy told me that he did not know I was Aunt Annie's brother. I will tell you this. Never will we loan any money to an individual again, even though that's not being compassionate. You do learn.

Speaking at the Field House

FOR THE TALK I gave at the University of Missouri Field House, I used the same speech I had used in Westphalia, only dropping off the improved pasture part and adding this:

> *We are here today because our fellow men elected us as leaders of our counties. As I look out upon the audience, I note many gray heads so I know that many of you recall the Depression and dust bowl years. I want each of you to call to mind someone who went out of his way to do something for you that was unexpected.*
>
> *I remember as a lad of 15 when my father died and after the closing of the old Cole County Bank and the estate sale we had nothing, not even a car. There were no aid plans in those days. We only had the Poor Farm and I can assure you that through my mother's determination we did not go there.*
>
> *My eldest brother, Carl, had moved to Tipton several years before and had taken over a loan of another who had failed as a farmer. He made quite a reputation for himself in farming and thereby was approached by an administrator of an estate asking if he wanted to rent more land.*
>
> *Carl thought about us and we decided to try to farm together, using most of his machinery plus the discarded machinery that my mother begged. We moved to Tipton on October 16, 1934, right in the face of winter. Things looked pretty bleak for the Mertens family.*
>
> *Then I remember the day when Mr. John Hainen, the*

administrator, came to our home and talked to my mother. This farm had a large home and big yard with many high black locust and maple trees. He said, "Mrs. Mertens, if your boys will help my son and me, we will trim those trees. It will make the estate sale better when we sell. You can have the wood for firewood" and so we had our winter's wood. I can also recall when he came down on a Saturday evening with a little Jersey cow on his truck and told my mother, "I don't know why I purchased this cow. Will you take care of her for me?" and we had milk to drink and lots of skim milk for gravy and soup. My mother skimmed off the cream and my brother and I carried that cream and live rabbits that we had caught the three miles to Tipton and the rabbits were shipped back East. Just enough money for flour, coffee, sugar, and lard.

I recall Mr. Phillip Imhoff who had a family of six and a Model T Ford car. This family stopped to take us to church on Sundays. How many people of today that you know would even stop and ask if an elderly person wanted to attend church?

I also remember Mr. Frank Lawson, who was road boss, asking my mother if we two boys would help him trim brush along the roadway. He said he had some cash money from those who did not want to work out their poll tax. We cut brush that winter and most was hedge and was all thorns. We were paid $.15 per hour.

My mother could take an egg and add flour to it and make what she called "egg butter" that we would spread on bread. I recall the many transients that traveled Highway 50 and many were dressed better than we and we would complain. Her answer was, "We have much to be thankful for. At least we have a home." She never turned anyone away without an egg butter sandwich.

As I stand here today as a dairyman, I have served on many committees and I ask myself why. It is then that I recall Mr. S.E. Lawson telling me how he and Bill Bower and several others worked so hard to begin the locally owned MFA Co-op that did three million dollars of business in California last year. Surely then I can take a day to be a delegate at the State Convention.

As a young man I can remember getting my first steady job from the Moniteau County Agricultural Association that Mr. Lawson began. This man became a second father to me and I tell myself if this *man can do so much for his community, then I at least can work with the many committees I serve on.*

Each time I turn on my automatic silo unloader I think again how Mr. Lawson, Mrs. Armin Hays, and others along with our old county agent, Fowler Young, did the footwork to form the Co-Mo Electric Cooperative. I recall how the farmers dug holes for the high line poles and then I tell myself don't complain of the needed legwork to form the Public Water Supply District and get dial telephones in our area. I just hope that I, along with those I worked with, can be remembered in the future as I remember those of yesteryear.

It seems that today we want to delegate our responsibility to another. "Let them do it" is our motto of today. So today I ask you to go back to your counties and work just as those before you. You can make your county a better place to live in and be proud of.

Ladies and gentlemen, I end with an old saying that I learned as a young boy. "No man is fit to be entrusted with the Present who is ignorant of the Past. No one who is indifferent to the Past need ever hope to make their Future." So today you can go home and accomplish many things and when you do you can be proud of those accomplishments and you can brag to others so that they can follow you. Thank you.

Several things stand out from that day. One, that I as an eighth-grade educated farmer was asked to stand before this group of people and state my principles. That I was received as an equal. As I did, I thought of Mom and Dad. Their "can do" spirit.

Two, a banker from Warsaw in Benton County came to me to shake my hand and said, "As you said, we can do those things. As a banker all I hear is negative."

Three, a man from Marshall in Saline County came up to me and told me, "I left Tipton 30 years ago and I still remember those people you spoke of."

Four, a lady from St. Charles County, Missouri came up to me and said, "When I saw the program for today I wondered who was this Mr. Mertens. Now I know. I just want to tell you that I am going home with an altogether different attitude than I came up here with."

Maybe I could be called a braggart, yet I walked away from that meeting feeling that I accomplished what I had come for. Needless to say, I was proud.

Epilogue

As I write this, my last chapter, I am in my 76th year. I certainly hope it was an enjoyable read. I could have written much more of those many things that took place throughout those many years but space did not permit it. I can only tell you that I would gladly re-live every year of them. I think many of us don't realize all the gifts God blessed us with that we should be thankful for. We also know that not everything in life can be a bed of roses and all of us can recall the many crosses we had to bear. All for the love of God.

My typewriter

So as I come to the end, Ida says, "Thank God. I'm getting tired of all the 'plunking' as you beat the typewriter to death." Well, it was given to me as a piece of junk by my son Ted and his clinic. He said let the grandkids play with it. Instead, I overhauled the old thing and three typewriter ribbons later it has completed my story. Just goes to show that old typewriters, like old men, never wear out and there will become a time we both will just fade away.

So I will say goodbye as I end and just until we meet again in writing. Remember to say a prayer for the old man. Think of Ida too.

We send our love until the end of time. Until we meet again.

- Bud

Acknowledgements

I'd like to thank Uncle Bud's children, David, Theodore, Karen, and Beverly, for allowing me to use his material as a basis for this book. Thanks to Beverly for welcoming me into her home to scan pictures. And I especially appreciate David's efforts in going through Uncle Bud's boxes to uncover precious family photos and helping me scan them all. It's an honor to share Uncle Bud's story.

Many thanks to my daughter, Vicki Lesage, for her careful and thorough editing, cover design, and general helpfulness in organizing the material.

I'd like to acknowledge my sister Mary Verner for collaborating with me on this project. Thanks for your hard work in locating and converting the original documents and photos.

I also want to acknowledge Quentin Veit, my dad, for all his contributions to this book and for being a great dad. I wish he was here so I could share this with him.

Ellen M. (Veit) Meyer, editor

A Note from the Editor

Dear Reader,

Thank you for taking the time to read *Back to the Country*. It has truly been a joy to edit this book and make it publicly available. Although the author, my great-uncle, wrote these stories over 30 years ago, the manuscript was recently rediscovered by my sisters and me. Reading Uncle Bud's stories gave me a sense of awe and pride, plus a few chuckles. I will always be grateful to him for leaving us this written legacy.

I hope you enjoyed *Back to the Country*. If so, I'd appreciate if you left a review on Amazon. Reviews help other readers decide to try out a new book. Just a sentence or two saying what you liked about the book will do!

You can read more of Bud's story in *Raised in the Country*, *Hard Times in the Country*, and *Serving My Country*.

If you enjoyed reading about the "old days," you'll love *The Bumpy Road*, where Bud's nephew Quentin Veit writes about growing up on a farm during the Great Depression.

Ellen M. (Veit) Meyer

Other Titles by Clement T. "Bud" Mertens

Raised in the Country: Memoir of a 1920s Childhood

Hard Times in the Country: Memoir of the 1930s Great Depression

Serving My Country: Memoir of a 1940s Stateside Soldier

Table of Illustrations

Lydia and Ida 8
1940s-era Dodge school bus 9
Ida and me when we were dating 10
Gerri and Ida 11
1941 ad for Nash 600 12
Cow on bridge [1] 13
Me with Lloyd Imhoff 16
Our wedding 19
Our Wedding party 20
Cousin Don Huhmann in front of honeymoon cabins 21
Stave bolts being unloaded from a wagon [2] 23
Emil, Cath, Ida, and me 27
Baby David 28
Glenn and Dorothy Tripp's wedding photo 30
Our first house 31
Me, Ida, and David 32
Ida and Darlene 33
Our house in Columbia 37
Ida's antique bed, now used by great-grandson Quentin [3] 38
Theodore, Karen, and David on the Plymouth 40
Baby Theodore 41
Dragline excavator 50
Bevier, Missouri coal mine 52
Missouri River flooding, Jefferson City, 1951 [4] 59
Baby Karen 61
David on toy tractor, Ted in wagon 68
Me and Ida 69
Tandem disc 75
Wheat drill 75
Ted, four years old 77
Panel truck school bus 79
Baby Beverly 80
David, Beverly, Karen, Ted, circa 1956 81
Hauling the old outhouse [5] 82
David's first communion 87
Cow stanchion 90
Vintage Studebaker pickup 96
1961 Ferguson 40 tractor 97

Brown Swiss cow [6]	99
Beverly, age three, feeding a calf	100
Holstein cow [7]	101
One of our registered heifers	102
Cows walking up steps	104
Elevated milking parlor	105
Pass-through from garage to cooler	112
Aerial view of farm with boundaries marked	115
List of acreage purchases	115
Our new manger	116
Our calves	121
Ida and me reviewing farm records with Dan McGrath, 1965	124
Our silo under construction	138
Dave and me spreading concrete, and Ida using rake	138
Ida, me, Beverly, Ted, Karen, David, circa 1970s.	142
Missouri State Farm Management Award	149
Newspaper article about our farm management award	151
Ida weighing feed	157
Newspaper article about our farm tours	159
Award-winning painting of house	165
Dave and Carolyn's wedding photo	167
Advertisement for the sale	171
Big Bend Basin	174
Angus bull [8]	180
Ted and Barb's wedding	189
Karen and Andrew's wedding	190
Picture frame with mementos	201
Ida	205
Baptism bib and sheet with fringe	210
Ida and me in our parish photo	211
Extension center award	215
My typewriter	233

Photo Credits

Photographs have been added to illustrate equipment, tools, locations, and people. Most of the new images are from family albums or are in the public domain. The exceptions are credited below.

1. Sketch by Stephen P. Monti, great-grand-nephew of the author.
2. Unloading stave bolts from wagon. National Archives and Records Administration, public domain, via Wikimedia Commons.
3. Photo courtesy of Jason and Keri Mertens. Note the quilt shown was made by Ida, and she also made the teddy bears from an old quilt of her grandmother's.
4. Missouri River flooding. The State Historical Society of Missouri, from the Otto and Joe Kroeger Photograph Collection.
5. Sketch by Victoria Lesage, great-grand-niece of the author.
6. Brown Swiss cow. Tiia Monto, CC BY-SA 3.0 <https://creativecommons.org/licenses/by-sa/3.0>, via Wikimedia Commons.
7. Holstein cow. Verum, CC BY-SA 3.0 <https://creativecommons.org/licenses/by-sa/3.0>, via Wikimedia Commons.
8. Angus bull. Gwen and James Anderson.
9. Sketch by Clement T. "Bud" Mertens.

Made in United States
Cleveland, OH
09 July 2025